Touch the Flame

Stories From The Okanagan Mountain Park Fire

Touch The Flame

Stories From The Okanagan Mountain Park Fire

Compiled by Jorie Soames and Glenna Turnbull

Northstone

Editors: Glenna Turnbull, Jim Couper, Kelly Dvorak
Cover and interior design: Verena Velten
Proofreading: Heather Picotte
Cover artwork: *There's Still Hope* acrylic on canvas (24" x 30") by Elizabeth Bologna

Northstone Publishing is an imprint of Wook Lake Books Inc.
Wood Lake Books acknowledges the financial support of the Government of Canada,
through the Book Publishing Industry Development Program (BPIDP)
for our publishing activities.

Wood Lake Books is an employee-owned company, committed to caring for the
environment and all creation. Wood Lake Books recycles, reuses, and encourages
readers to do the same. Resources are printed on recycled paper and more
environmentally friendly groundwood papers (newsprint), whenever possible.
The trees used are replaced through donations to the Scoutrees For Canada Program.
A percentage of all profit is donated to charitable organizations.

Library and Archives Canada Cataloguing in Publication

Touch the flame: stories from the Okanagan Mountain Park Fire /
compiled by Jorie Soames and Glenna Turnbull.

ISBN 1-896836-68-2

1. Forest fires – British Columbia – Okanagan Mountain Park – Anecdotes. 2. Forest
fires – British Columbia – Kelowna Region – Anecdotes. 3. Fires – British Columbia
– Okanagan Mountain Park – Anecdotes. 4. Fires – British Columbia – Kelowna Region
– Anecdotes. 5. Okanagan Mountain Park (B.C.) – History – Anecdotes. 6. Kelowna
Region (B.C.) – History – Anecdotes. I. Soames, Jorie II. Turnbull, Glenna III. Title.
SD421.34.C3T69 2004   363.37'9   C2004-903276-3

Published by Northstone Publishing
an imprint of Wood Lake Books, Inc.
9025 Jim Bailey Road, Kelowna, BC, Canada, V4V 1R2
250.766.2778 • www.northstone.com

Printing 10 9 8 7 6 5 4 3 2 1
Printed in Canada

DEDICATION

In memory of pilots Eric Ebert, Ian Mackay, and Ben von Hardenberg, who lost their lives fighting fires near Cranbrook and Boneparte Lake as true heroes of the firestorms, summer of 2003.

ACKNOWLEDGEMENTS

We wish to thank the many people who helped make this book happen
with their practical help, resources, and council.

Thank you to:
Allen Arndt of RDA Art Investments, Cindy Aspden, Blair Sportswear, Marg Boyd, Ed Brouwer of Canwest
Fire, Terry Chaffee, Gord Grisenthwaite, Michael Kerr, Charlie McClelland of Tiger Press, New Beginnings
Community Church, Okanagan Freelance Writers Group, Mike Roberts of CHBC, Amy Scovil-Lashinski,
Tom Soames, Sharon Thiesen, Randy Zahara.

A big thank you to TTF staff for many hours of volunteer work, sweat, and tears,
and especially to their families for giving them time to pursue this passion.

Thank you to our co-sponsors for believing in this project:
Capital News, Kelowna and District Arts Council, Salvation Army, 101 Silk FM.

Thank you Wood Lake Books/Northstone Publishing for your generosity
in providing the community with this beautiful book.

CREDITS

TTF Staff: Jim Couper – Consulting Editor

Kelly Dvorak – Children's and Poetry Editor

Deborah Matheson – Assistant Project Coordinator

Jorie Soames – Project Coordinator

Glenna Turnbull – Senior Editor

Verena Velten – Book Design

Photography: Don Case *(page 20)*

Cpl. William. C. Gomm *(pages 6, 106, 116, 142)*

Ken Levert *(pages 167, 176)*

Glenna Turnbull *(pages 5, 37, 38, 53, 62, 70, 87,105,123,124,141,148,159,168, 175)*

Mike Schwartzentruber *(page 54)*

Cover: Acrylic Painting by Elizabeth Bologna, *There's Still Hope*.

Photography by Cpl. William. C. Gomm *(frontcover)* and Glenna Turnbull *(backcover)*

TABLE OF CONTENTS

INTRODUCTION

During the summer of 2003, over 2,400 fires burned 267,000 hectares in British Columbia.

On August 16th, lightning struck in Okanagan Mountain Park some 20 kilometres from the city of Kelowna, and 17 kilometres from the little town of Naramata. Within days a forest fire grew to 10,000 hectares, threatening both town and city. If the wind blew one way, Naramata was spared. If the wind turned, Kelowna was spared. For a time it seemed the flames would devour both.

On August 22nd, a rank six fire storm raced through the southern neighbourhoods of Kelowna, heading north along the eastern border at a speed of approximately 50 metres per minute.

Army and Navy troops deployed to Kelowna, joining the sixty-five fire departments from B.C. and Alberta, over 1,000 Ministry of Forest firefighters, 250 pieces of heavy equipment, 50 air tankers, water bombers and helicopters in the battle against the flames. The second largest evacuation in Canada took place, displacing 30,000 people from their homes. The Kelowna City Emergency Plan was activated with close to 1,500 trained volunteers from various agencies working under the banner of Emergency Social Services. Two evacuation centres were set up: one at Parkinson Recreation Centre and one at Kelowna Senior Secondary School.

An amazing story of human history unfolded, involving the citizens of the Okanagan Valley, thousands of guests, and millions of worried onlookers the world over. In total 25,912 hectares of treed forests, parkland, recreational areas, and residential neighbourhoods burned. The beloved Kettle Valley Railroad lost 12 of its 18 trestles. The homes of 238 Kelowna families were destroyed. Though firefighters were injured, and some trapped behind flames, no lives were lost to this fire.

This book captures that moment in history. The people's own voices record thoughts, feelings, and events as the fire races through forests and neighbourhoods alike.

Brought together by their desire to see these stories told, local writers sparked the idea of a community project using writing as a form of healing. A selection committee read through over 130 submissions, choosing voices for *Touch the Flame*. Many individuals took up the flame, volunteering countless hours to make this book a true reflection of an area that cares about its people, about its land, its history, and about how we interact with the rest of the world.

Jorie Soames

Project Coordinator

May 19, 2004

A forest fire came roaring out of Okanagan Mountain Park in August 2003 and invaded the neighbourhoods on the south boundary of our beautiful city. Temperatures of 2,000° heat evaporated 238 houses and diminished others. The evacuations that preceded the devastating fire were the second largest in Canadian history.

Kelowna will celebrate forever that no lives were lost, as well-trained emergency crews and volunteers came to the rescue. Nearly one-third of Kelowna's population was evacuated. Some of them twice.

Even though "horrific and devastating," history will show that Firestorm 2003 was a turning point in the development and evolution of Kelowna – and especially its people.

The fire is now history. But, as a community, we all now know

- *who we are and the stuff we're made of,*

- *the courage we have and the compassion we demonstrate,*

- *and the resolve we mustered to come out of all of this better and stronger as a community.*

And now come the stories. Some are humourous. Some are simply for the record. Many are of courage as ordinary citizens did extraordinary things for people and the Kelowna they love.

Yours very truly,

Walter Gray

MAYOR, City of Kelowna

Chapter One
Standing Ground

"Not really much of a story to tell other than it was the closest thing to war that I hope I will ever be near. I am sure glad we could help out and that no lives were lost."

NEIL WALTON - PILOT, DC6 TANKER 450, YUKON GROUP

"You couldn't pay me enough to do what they do, but they aren't thinking of the money. They aren't thinking they are heroes. They are thinking of nothing but doing what they have to do. That is a hero."

SHEILA CHATTEN

WE KNOW THE RISKS: WE STAY BY SHER ALCOCK, SUNSHINE FARM

The fire is so close, we are under one hour evacuation order. Our grown children arrive to help; we are all in disbelief that anything could threaten our home. The farm is our sanctuary; the kids grew up on its meadows, playing in its ponds, running through the trees. Sunshine Farm is the site for vocational programs for adults in the Community Living Sector - it means so much to so many.

Out the front window we realize things are changing rapidly. Saucier Road, usually quiet, has become a steady parade of horse trailers, bicycles, cattle liners, trucks, and campers. People are leaving; by vehicle, on horseback, some leading other horses, moving farm animals and belongings as quickly as they can. Speeding vehicles set the frantic tempo.

The TV confirms it – the fire is closing in on Kelowna's south slopes. In shock, we understand that we are to evacuate. We prepare to leave and with almost no discussion, decide to stay. Within an hour people fill our house. Staff, family, and friends load boxes with anything they think we might need or want. The help is incredible. We load the truck and all available vehicles with photos, hard drives, personal treasures, whatever we can think of and leave keys in the ignition. We are ready to flee and prepared to stay. After the packing is done and the roadblocks go up, there are eight of us with no opportunity to plan, shop, or leave. To cross the roadblock would mean no return.

We fill every container with water, unsure of a steady supply. The chlorinators have been removed from our district to avoid fire damage. Every available bucket on the farm is filled with water and these are placed strategically across the land with a towel, bathmat, coat, whatever to give us a quick 'wet blanket' to throw on a fire. Hoses are laid out to every tinder-dry corner.

Our protection against a wall of flame is the pasture behind us. We worry about keeping ashes, bark and debris raining on the farm from igniting a fire. Our efforts over this blistering summer to keep water use to a minimum are forgotten. Every sprinkler is in use. Outbuildings are dripping as though in a rain. Barrels of water wait in the front-end loader, a quick way to move water to any corner of 12.5 acres. Lars climbs the large tree beside the house and ties on a 70-foot rope. The chainsaw rests at the base, ready to take it out if we must. This tree shades the house in summer, held the kids' tire swing, held the antenna during our son's CB radio years and shields our hot tub from the rain and snow. The tree becomes our signal, if it starts to burn, we all leave, right away!

Two lookout stations with chairs and blankets are used for a 24-hour fire watch. No one sleeps. The power goes out. We check the generator. Tired brains scramble. What will we need to keep going if it does not come back? Will we lose water pressure? How long can the freezers go before they need topping up - can we keep the neighbours freezers going? Candles are everywhere, but with the fire blazing behind us, lighting a candle becomes almost an act of aggression. Thankfully the power is out for only a couple of hours.

On Friday the wind blows the flames around the mountain, no longer a faint line but with the face of a monster. The flames are immense, the fire blasting along the mountain, jumping, running ahead of itself in a demonic glee, defying even the darkness of the night. The mountain leaps in flame, glowers and roars from top to bottom, east to west.

We stand in a row, gagged with bandanas against the choking smoke and listening in shock to the explosions of houses in the Crawford subdivision. I don't know what explodes when a house burns – propane tanks, vehicles? – but the sound of hundreds of houses burning at once brings a feeling of catastrophe and chills your spine with your mortality. The ashes and debris falling on the fields are now mixed with bits of houses, vinyl siding and unidentifiable burned scraps.

The fire reaches the end of Stewart Road on the corner and Stan's house goes up. The sense of helplessness is overwhelming. I never truly understood the term firestorm before this night, but will always envision those huge, fast moving, twisting flames when I hear it now. Lightning strikes. On the fifth strike the wind subsides. Incredulously it starts to rain. The rain does not come close to dousing the fire but quells it for a time, giving us a break. The smoke descends. We are exhausted, spent.

In the morning our sons peddle their bikes over to Stan's house and try to collect the cat. Unable to catch him they leave food and use buckets of water to put out the fence posts where flames still flicker under the trees. The house, completely incinerated, is a charred chimney on an ash-covered concrete pad, nothing else. Absurdly, a stack of hay 20 or 30 feet from the house is intact.

At the farm a police officer pulls in, respectful, concerned. This is not the first request that we leave. Our stock reply is that we truly appreciate the concern and know the risks. We are ready to go if needed. He tells us that our escape routes may be blocked – we assure him we understand. He looks so tired. The nights are spent in uneasy rotation of watching and sleeping.

Coughing, we wake up, it's 4 a.m. The bedroom is thick with smoke and Jon is groping for bandanas. If the fire doesn't drive us out, the smoke might. We wrap the bandanas around our faces, bury our heads back under the covers and try to sleep.

For days we watch the mountain burn; the helicopters and water bombers create a constant din. Truck after truck of military and heavy equipment driving around us to the mountain. There is a great sense of security having them there. We feel that while they are there at least someone is nearby watching. Amazing – it becomes normal to look out the window and see flames, to have the night lit up with flashes of fire, to live in constant smoke.

After more than a week of lockdown the evacuation order is lifted to a one hour alert and our neighbours start to return. There is no joy here, everyone is subdued. We are still under one hour evacuation, the smoke is still thick, the air is still a choreograph of planes and choppers, the mountain is still flaring up. It's an uneasy time for everyone. Our children leave to carry on with their lives; our family has shown its strength with the ability to drop everything and do what it takes to pull together.

We are emotional about this fire to this day. We still walk up the mountain but now it is through acres of charred trees. There are areas where seemingly nothing lives, but in spring, now, there are tiny blades of grass, small spring bulbs pushing up through the ash. And yesterday, in the midst of a burn, I saw two butterflies. It really will be okay, the forest will, in time, return. Mother Nature takes her hand and blows new life into her own devastation.

FIRESTORM by Ruth Chambers

First there was the lightning

In the middle of the night

Reminding us of nature's

Ever powerful might

Suddenly the fire, which started as a flame

Triumphed over lesser man, and

Oppressed our domain

Razing homes and all within, and now

Memories are all that remain

You're Our Hero!

Mitch Brown's story as told to and written by Pamela Irving

We were there from the very first, when lightning hit across from Rattlesnake Island, to the very end on September 15. It was only 60 hectares to start, just a little fire; we didn't think it would go anywhere. In the weeks to come, helicopters got pulled in from across Canada, everything from the very biggest Chinooks and Sky Cranes, to little Jet Rangers used for fire mapping. Bell 212's are somewhere in between.

My job was to bucket water from a "longline." The buckets may look small in the air but they have a 350 gallon capacity. We worked 14-hour days, double crewing. Pilot Tyler Hupp and I rotated each other off. One of us would start at dawn, fly for seven or eight hours, then switch out and the next guy would fly until the end of the day. There is a very strict flight duty roster. Though the hours were long, we always took the proper time off for safety.

People wonder how the whole operation hangs together, how the pilots know where to go. There is a chopper called a "bird dog' with a Forestry worker who maps the fire from the air. He determines where the hottest spots are and the points of greatest danger to people. If a fire is just going to burn off in the bush somewhere and another one is threatening peoples' homes, they will send us to the latter. Fires that threaten homes and communities are called interface fires. This was my first interface fire.

The bird dog relays the information about the fires and that's how we know where to bucket. There are up to five aircraft bucketing water at a time. The turn around time can be up to 35 minutes depending on where the source of water is relative to the fire.

We bucket within 20 feet of the shoreline, using it as a guide. We get into a circuit of mutual frequency. We didn't always use the lake. In Crawford Estates we used a guy's pool as a bucket site. We can get the bucket into very specific targets with tight parameters.

The ground was particularly hot and dry. Usually you can see a wet line where you fly to drop the water. Not here. The water evaporated before we could come back for another drop. That's very unusual.

The biggest challenge of fighting the fires is the smoke and visibility. We must maintain a visual reference with the ground at all times. If we can't see through the smoke, we don't go in. If someone calls out "clear the smoke" on the radio, we know to wait. You're only in the thickest smoke for about 30 seconds so we learn how to breathe through it as we don't use smoke masks. It can taste nasty!

It was awesome to see how the community came together. We don't think of it much when we are protecting a stand of timber but when you are protecting somebody's home, it sends a chill down your spine.

We had an air conditioned RV where we could take a break and get a drink of water. One day, I had just gone inside when someone came in and said, "There's someone outside who wants to talk to a pilot." I told him to send the person in and a little boy, just nine years old, came in. He asked me, "Are you the pilot of that helicopter out there?" I said, "I sure am." He grinned the biggest grin and asked, "Can I have your autograph? You're our heroes!" I was touched. I thought I was just doing my job and to this little guy I was a hero. So I gave him my autograph. He asked if I knew where he could find another pilot because he wanted the autographs of all the pilots. I was happy to oblige and pointed him over to a buddy. He said, "You guys have the coolest job." It leaves such a smile on your face to see a kid light up like that.

Once, a guy and his wife drove up in a mini van. They opened the back of their van and they had fresh sandwiches and fruit for us. I tell you, to have a fresh sandwich made for you is pretty special. People were doing stuff like that all the time.

I think it's good to talk to people about our experiences and what we do. Education is very necessary, especially with what happened here. One day, I was sitting in Tim Horton's. A guy spotted my Wildcat sticker on my truck and asked if I was fighting the fires. When I told him I was a pilot bucketing water, he raced to his truck and got out some radio equipment. It turned out he was from Sun FM so I talked to him. Guys back at Wildcat were laughing when they heard their buddy Mitch on the air but it's important to let the public know what's going on. Little things, like how much water a bucket holds, the public doesn't know. It helps them understand the whole operation better.

There are reasons for everything in an operation like this and everybody involved, from management on the ground like Gerry Zimmermann, to people in the air. People say, "This should never happen again," and it shouldn't. But realistically, with stands of timber near towns that haven't been logged or selectively burnt, it's going to happen again, not just here, but across Canada. People have to be willing to pay to have helicopters at ready. It costs $2,500 per hour to operate a Bell 212, and that doesn't include the 400 litres of fuel. It includes the costs of all the support staff and pilots. It's not cheap, but it's necessary.

We were bucketing water right up until September 15, putting out spot fires. There are ground fires still spreading even now, six months later, but people need to know that it's contained. It's under control.

My wife with our two small children decided to make Kelowna our home last spring. Then the fire happened over the summer. My wife had a few second thoughts while the fires raged, but we like it here and we're going to stay. It's a great place to live and a great community.

Journal of a Reserve Soldier

by Captain Chris Mullins, 6 Field Engineer Squadron, North Vancouver

AUGUST 21 - Reservists arriving in Vernon from all parts of Western Canada go through a process of medical examinations, interviews and paperwork (completing wills and notification of next of kin forms) and are assigned to a composite reserve infantry company.

AUGUST 22 - At the conclusion of our one-day training session, firefighting equipment is issued. We do not know that the Okanagan Mountain fire is raging out of control. A decision is made to bus us to Kelowna so we go directly to the Lakeshore Road area.

AUGUST 23 (SATURDAY, 2 A.M.) - We witness an eerie scene like something out of *Dante's Inferno* with beautiful new homes burning in every direction we look. As we move through many parts of Lakeshore Road in those early morning hours, I notice that the fire did not destroy every home or every stand of trees. The plan therefore is for my reservists, along with another regular army company, to spread out and protect those homes, property, and trees left standing. What an odd sight to look down these streets with their beautifully manicured lawns and see 20 to 30 fires flickering in the darkness all around us. We employ big water tanker trucks with pumps and fire hoses and as these vehicles slowly advance down each street, my soldiers drag the fire hoses up driveways – sometimes finding nothing more than a chimney and the cement foundation. Next morning, after 30 hours without sleep, military vehicles move my exhausted soldiers to an army field camp being set up in a sports field. What amazes all of us during the move through Kelowna and over the next 12 days is the townspeople who wave, cheer, clap, and honk their horns in appreciation. For many reservists it is the first time that their dedication to serve as part-time soldiers is appreciated by the public. Over the following three days my soldiers put out countless fires that threaten homes. The majority of work involves scaling steep, rocky embankments, dragging hundreds of metres of fire hose and attempting to douse fires and hotspots. Fortunately we have no shortage of water as the pump system we set up leads to Okanagan Lake.

AUGUST 25 - We continue to protect empty homes and vineyards. The biggest challenge is the dryness here. As we focus on small fires in one area, other fires start behind us from embers floating in the air or flames resurfacing from root systems burning underground. This makes progress slow and frustrating, as each morning numerous hotspots are found in areas we had previously extinguished. I constantly remind my soldiers of escape routes if the wind changes and the fire turns on us. Each soldier knows our safety zone – run down the hill and into Okanagan Lake to wait for rescue or wait out the fire. Each day starts at 5 a.m. and we work 12 hour shifts on the fire-line. Work is intense and my soldiers eat four meals each day (two lunches, one at 11:30 a.m., one at 4 p.m., then supper at 8 p.m. on our return to camp).

AUGUST 26 - We have been assigned an area farther up the mountain and farther east from the lake. A power line and another community of new homes are under threat. The plan of attack for my platoon (39 soldiers) is to spread out along this power line and advance into a forest, extinguishing every hotspot or fire we find (called mopping-up). Strange as it is, most of the trees remain standing but the ground looks like powder snow as a thick layer of ash is everywhere. The roots of many pine trees continue to burn. A danger to my soldiers comes from the possibility of the ground giving way beneath them. Our work involves digging open roots to expose hot coals, hosing them down, raking them over and repeating the process.

AUGUST 27 - As we advance deeper and extinguish hotspots, a major fire rages 500 to 700 metres east of our position. Although much of the work is straightforward and almost boring, the wind changes in mid-afternoon and those small fires intensify. The military officers leading platoons on either side of us assess the threat as too dangerous and abandon their positions. Upon hearing this I increase the number of fire observers. We continue putting out fires and when they become too large, helicopters with water buckets come overhead and put them out – occasionally dousing some of my soldiers.

AUGUST 29-30 - The effort has paid off and only small fires flare up. Each time we return to camp we see an increasing number of homemade signs of every description expressing thanks to all the firefighters. It truly is a good feeling, witnessing such tremendous support from the community.

AUGUST 31 - We are now among the most experienced military firefighters and so are dispatched to a new fire at Vaseux Lake.

SEPTEMBER 2 - Again, no water except what my soldiers carry in "squirt cans." Our area is a kilometre from the road but climbs 600 feet. We carry up a collapsible 1,500-litre bladder, in the hope water will arrive. I gain the attention of a helicopter and point to our empty bladder. Ten minutes later two large helicopters arrive overhead with huge buckets dangling below. My soldiers grab the water bladder and hold it open. These pilots are amazing as they gingerly swing 3,000 pound buckets inches over our heads and lower them into the bladder before releasing their contents. Now we are ready to do some serious damage.

SEPTEMBER 6 - After 14 days of continuous fire fighting, we get two days off for rest and relaxation in Vernon. Many reservists are students and must begin classes so they head home.

SEPTEMBER 8 - I organize what is left of the reserve company and move them by military bus to the Chase fire near Kamloops.

SEPTEMBER 15 - My time is up and my reserve company is broken into two large platoons and attached to other composite infantry companies. I am sent to Camp Vernon for out-processing, issued a bus ticket home and my adventure as a firefighter comes to an end.

For the 700 reservists who came here from all parts of Western Canada, this experience had a profound effect on their lives – even for those who had witnessed the effects of war during peacekeeping operations overseas. For most of these part-time soldiers this was their first operational experience and in helping so many fellow citizens during the summer of 2003, they each came to understand the importance of the decision they made years earlier in choosing to join Canada's reserve army.

Saved by Eight Feet
by Doris Tonn

On a very smoky Tuesday, August 19, I returned from my volunteer job at the Kelowna General Hospital to find a notice on my door which read "Evacuation Alert." It gave me a very uneasy feeling and I went about packing a few of our important files, pictures, and some souvenirs from various parts of the world. We were able to store these items in our son's condo down in Kelowna.

Since the air was so thick with smoke in the Upper Mission, we were not able to sleep in our bedroom even with all the windows shut. The downstairs was a bit more comfortable and that is where we spent the next couple of nights. On Wednesday we decided to take a few more items down to Kelowna for safekeeping. The following day we took a walk in Belcarra Estates and one of the fire inspectors mentioned that we were relatively safe because the fire was heading towards Naramata, which did not comfort us very much because my brother and his family live in that community.

We stopped in on an acquaintance on Stellar and he mentioned that the fire bombers had turned their attention from the Belcarra Estates to the area behind Kettle Valley, which was rather unnerving because now they were flying over our house on Okaview.

As I walked into the kitchen to start making supper, I turned on the TV for the latest information on the fire and saw flashing across the screen, "Okaview being evacuated immediately." I thought this must be a mistake because no one had come to our door and things seemed rather calm at this point. I rushed over to the window and saw our neighbours hurriedly carrying items to their cars. At that point our relatives called from Naramata and expressed their concern that we were being evacuated. In a matter of three minutes we were out of the house with a few grocery items in order to make supper at our son's place. The drive down the hill into Kelowna took all of ten minutes because we were among the first to take the evacuation order seriously.

The following night we watched the fire from our son's balcony. It was definitely raging in our neighbourhood in the Upper Mission. It was difficult to watch but we stayed calm. Then, all of a sudden, the fire died down and it became totally dark in that area. Our immediate thought was, "it must be pouring there," although only a couple of drops fell where we were staying. Kelowna churches had opened their doors for people to come and pray for rain and although many homes were lost, we believe many more would have been lost if the rain had not come at that point.

On Friday night we had already made arrangements to drive to Merritt to get away from the pollution in Kelowna, but at the very last moment, I felt compelled to stay in town. I now believe that was a good choice because we were able to find out Sunday afternoon at the Trinity Baptist Church that our home had been miraculously spared. Our son took a boat ride with a friend along the shoreline and with binoculars, saw our home. It was reassuring to know we had a house to come home to.

Right next to our property is a vacant lot with many tall ponderosa pines and a lot of very tall dry grass immediately next to our wooden fence. My husband took a couple of hours to clean about eight feet wide along the whole depth of that property just hours before we were evacuated and when we returned to our home after the evacuation order was lifted, the fire had attacked everything on the other side of the eight feet of that property but touched absolutely nothing on the cleared area. Many people observed this distinct line and were convinced that the effort my husband put in saved our property.

We will always be grateful to our family and friends for their support and offers of help, and of course, to the firefighters who saved so very many homes. Our appreciation and gratitude will always be theirs. One cannot bestow enough praise on the very well organized disaster program that exists in our wonderful City of Kelowna. They certainly had an opportunity to shine, and during this terrible disaster, the volunteers did a wonderful job.

Code Three

by Andrew Speed

I'm a computer systems technologist at Malaspina University College but I am also a volunteer firefighter with the Errington Fire Department near Parksville, Vancouver Island, where I have been Assistant Fire Chief for five of the past 10 years.

On Monday, August 18, the B.C. Fire Commissioner's Office calls our station to request assistance with the wild fires that are threatening southern B.C. and, in particular, the Okanagan Mountain Fire which has increased enormously in the few days since it began as a lightning strike. The commissioner says homes are already being threatened.

We very quickly assemble a crew of three firefighters, prepare the truck and make our way to the ferry. The commissioner's office calls us again to say the fire is moving so rapidly that we should proceed with Code Three status over the Coquihalla — lights and sirens on, all the way to Kelowna. Code Three is not necessary, as there is no traffic, and 110 kph is about as fast as we like to run the apparatus.

As we descend into Kelowna at 4 a.m. we can see the orange glow from 30 kilometres away. We anticipate heading straight into the fire zone but are told to catch a few hours sleep and then report to Station 1 early in the morning.

On Wednesday we are instructed to tour the areas of Kelowna that are threatened by the fires and to familiarize ourselves with the streets, planning escape routes in case things go bad.

Kettle Valley is our staging area and when we drive our engine there we are overwhelmed by homeowners seeking information from us. Little do they know how little we know.

On Thursday, the out-of-town crews are split into two 12-hour shifts. We are pleased that we draw the day shift. What on earth are we thinking? By 10 a.m. we are mopping up at the end of Lakeshore Road and protecting the "big white house." At 7 p.m. we are back at the station anticipating some sleep when pandemonium breaks loose.

We lead the convoy of trucks through Kelowna back to the Kettle Valley subdivision. A running crown fire, several kilometres in length, is heading towards the subdivision. In spite of the steady stream of traffic making its way down the only exit road, we make it up the hill without any trouble.

Our engine is equipped with a compressed air foam system so we lay a foam guard around the perimeter of the subdivision. At 10:30 p.m. we are re-deployed back to Lakeshore Road, where the fire is burning down to the water and we spend the rest of the night protecting homes and fighting the pockets of fire.

At 5 a.m. most of the larger fires are out so we return to our hotel looking forward to some rest, but by 11 a.m. we are back on Lakeshore Road putting out hotspots and providing support for forestry back burn operations.

By 1 p.m. the winds pick up and small fires begin to grow very quickly. Matters get out of hand quickly as the fire races across Lakeshore to Bertram Creek Park and cuts off our escape route. The flames are more than 100 feet high. We remain boxed in at the end of Lakeshore for a few hours till the fire subsides enough to travel back towards Uplands.

We stage in the Uplands area where at 3 p.m. the houses are beginning to burn. We are told to leave that area as well. We set off once again to Kettle Valley where we spend the rest of the afternoon and evening fighting spot fires and houses that were just starting to burn. At 9 p.m. we are fighting huge fires in the subdivisions. We make a stand with two other engines and set off with our hoses through the backyards. At one point I burst through a thick hedge only to almost land in a swimming pool. As I look around and realize I am alone, the scene is surreal. All the homes across the street and to the left of me are fully involved. High winds continue to whip the flames, helicopters soar overhead and the memory of those moments will always be my own *Apocalypse Now*.

We spend the rest of the night protecting homes. At 5 a.m. we are relieved and make our way back to our hotel. At 10 a.m. we are back at the fire station and see that 20 more trucks have arrived. A couple of fellows from New Westminster come with us out to the Okaview and Curlew area where we can see the carnage in the daylight. Again, the sight is surreal.

By Sunday there are about 100 fire rigs at the station and after one more trip out Lakeshore to seek out hot spots, we are relieved by our replacements from Errington.

I check my watch to see if we can catch the last ferry back to the Island so we can sleep in our own beds for the first time in a week, with the hope that the worst has passed for the residents of Kelowna.

Yes to Both Questions

**by Brigadier-General J.I. Fenton, Commander,
Land Force Western Area and Commander, Task Force Peregrine**

On Saturday, 2 August, we received the call: British Columbia was enduring an epidemic of forest fires, the B.C. Forest Service was over-stretched, available firefighters from other provinces had been called and the continuing hot, dry weather indicated that the worst was to come. Could the Army send troops to help fight the fires?

My liaison officer in Victoria, Captain Steve Newman, answered my two essential questions: were available civilian resources outstripped by the crisis, and did the fires truly represent a significant risk to the lives and livelihood of Canadians? Yes to both questions.

Within hours, lead elements of B Company, First Battalion, Princess Patricia's Canadian Light Infantry (1 PPCLI) were on their way from Edmonton to join the fight at the Barriere/McLure fire. They and the thousands of troops who would follow, first underwent emergency training in fighting forest fires under B.C. Forest Service trainers. All troops were issued safety hats and gloves and fire resistant coveralls. As the situation continued to deteriorate, successive requests for more troops caused me to establish our headquarters and logistics base at the Army Cadet Camp in Vernon. As the rising number of troops began to overtax the logistics capacity of the fire service, we deployed not only firefighters, but also troops to feed, transport, and provide medical and all logistic support for military firefighters. Soon we had four battalion-size task forces working for incident commanders at four different fires.

Our biggest troop concentration was against the Okanagan Mountain Park Fire. Here, Lieutenant-Colonel Denis Cyr, Commanding Officer of the Reserve regiment British Columbia Dragoons (based in Kelowna and in Vernon), commanded a large task force of Regular and Reserve soldiers. The worst crisis struck on 22 August, while we were still early in our deployment. On that dreadful night B Company of 1 PPCLI, now on its second deployment to the fire zone, fought with a newly-arrived company of Reserve soldiers from across British Columbia beside the B.C. Forest Service and the Kelowna Fire Department to save as many houses as possible. Few of us will forget the sight of thousands of evacuees fleeing the roaring wall of flame that swept into the suburbs. Staff and volunteers under the aegis of the Provincial Emergency Program performed Herculean tasks this night and for many subsequent days to help families through the emergency. For many of my soldiers, the conditions of that night in particular brought back memories of tragedies we have seen in far off countries.

I spent a lot of time over our six-week deployment visiting troops on the fire line. Without exception, they told me they were glad to be helping their fellow Canadians. While many had served several tours of duty overseas and had witnessed terrible man-made tragedies and suffering, they were deeply touched to see fellow citizens caught up in the turmoil of a natural disaster. Some of my soldiers were from British Columbia, and were truly "close to home." Many other soldiers had never been in B.C. before, and were seeing the Okanagan for the first time: these, in particular, often told me they were going to come back and visit this beautiful part of our country in a more peaceful time.

Passing over skeletal remains of forests and black-stained mountains, flying through the pall of gigantic smoke clouds, we could not help being awed by the strength and speed of the fires. Flying over the burnt-out remains of houses, chimneys standing black against the sky looked eerily similar to what many of us had witnessed in the Balkans, where similar destruction was caused by the murderous acts of neighbour against neighbour.

My soldiers and I were glad we were able to help fellow Canadians in a time of need. We were moved by the courage, the kind words of thanks, and the resolute spirit of everyone determined to get through this together and carry on. We were also impressed by the professionalism and dedication demonstrated by the B.C. Forest Service, the staff and volunteers of the Provincial Emergency Program and the police. The satisfaction of working with a fine team to combat an enemy of tremendous ferocity and power will be a memory to treasure forever.

VOICE OF MYRA CANYON

You've called me "Myra" — once the name
That Newman[1] gave to daughter cherished,
And to a station, sidings, yard
That once met trains, but now have vanished.

For once I was a proud hostess
To a railway
Through our tortuous land
Of azure lakes, green forests tall,
And buried wealth that lured you all.

With long debate and lurking doubt,
In nineteen ten, you despatched out
McCulloch's[2] engineering host.
"From Coast to Kootenays" was your boast.

From Midway west, east from Penticton,
'Tween Kettle Valley and the Lake,
'Cross massive ridge and on your maps drawn,
Strings of survey lines did snake.

And when my chasm you did see,
You pondered how to deal with me.
Some said, "Yes," while others, "No."
"Let's go around." "Let's build down low,
Through fair Kelowna's orchard land."
But bold McCulloch raised his hand.

He placed around my emerald nape
A necklace
Strung with iron rails,
And for its jewels he set aloft
What engineering skill entails:
Along firm roadbed, 'neath my edge —
Eighteen trestles, two of steel,
A pair of tunnels — seemed not real!

Through numerous years,
The trains came creeping,
With throttles low, and wheels shrieking,
Along my gaping, cavernous throat.
And from the heights, down through my moat,
I sent you streams, from melting snow,
That watered thirsty engines black
And homes and orchards far below.

But then, in time, the trains were gone
To gentler and less costly grade.
Said CPR, "Since there's no trade,
Remove the rails, uproot the ties,
And then we'll see what value lies."

But you did not much time need take,
For swiftly in the Railway's wake,
Because my marvels you'd beheld
Even 'fore the Railway's yen had failed,
You saved my trestles, smoothed my bed,
Drove vehicles, or walked instead
Around my lips.
And as your wonders did accrue,
You asked in awe,
"Is all this true?"

You organized your interest strong,
You blocked my roadbed at both ends,
So only stout pedestrians,
Or cyclists could my joys behold,
And save me damages foretold.

You planked my trestles, set guardrail,
Erected plaques, tamped down the trail,
You sang my praise in many lands,
And tourists came in growing bands.

[1] J. L. Newman was assistant engineer during the construction of the Kettle Valley Railway.
[2] Andrew McCulloch (1864-1945) was the Chief Engineer, later Superintendent, of the Kettle Valley Railway during its most critical construction years. He is recognized as having been one of the most brilliant locating surveyors in the history of Canadian railroading.

BY LES FALK

And as my fame the world did stride,
You shared, with me, a burgeoning pride.
And high officials took my measure,
Proclaiming me historic treasure!

But then there came a fear-fraught season,
In that sad year, two thousand three.
Through rain-starved land (and for that reason)
A monster fire
Came raging free.

It came from far, near curve of Lake,
Left desolate park in its grim wake,
It torched fine homes,
Charred countless trees,
Cavorted devilishly in strong breeze,
And taking a gargantuan path,
It sent you fleeing from its wrath.

And when it played at half-asleep,
Up loftier slopes did boldly creep
Its right-hand claw.
It crossed the Kettle Valley line,
Climbed sister Bellevue's[3] east incline,
Then, roaring down from high plateau,
Invaded me.

Brave fire crews cried, "How can we keep
This priceless treasure from the sweep
Of this consuming, hideous blaze?
For if we leave, 'twill surely raze,
From ancient creosoted heap."

But though they tried preventive art,
They finally said, "We must depart!"
For my topography's too steep
For hose and manpower to leap.

For four long days, I heard you sigh,
"Could her destruction now be nigh?"
Twelve wooden trestles turned to smoke,
And wooden planking on the metal
Fell down to ash around my hem —
The flames, they were too much for them.

And when the smoke at last did clear,
Stood four survivors, now held dear.

Now here I lie, though not alone,
My trees are scorched, most trestles gone.
But through the mists, I bid you cheer,
My dearest friends, for I'm still here!

My roadbed's good, foundations strong,
Four trestles live, should you take long
To reconstruct my cherished site?
For once you did, with bold foresight,
Create it.

If such is what you will to do,
With open arms, I'll welcome you!

Then you'll return from far and near,
And my soul's secret clearly hear.
For it can never be confused
That in me both of these are fused:
Within one single, sweeping sight —
Great works of Man,
And Nature's might.

And from my depths, this would I say,
An affirmation like no other:
This truth — we have a common mother.

For we both do most clearly see
That Nature made both you and me.

[3] Bellevue Canyon lies to the southwest of Myra Canyon. Although a similar geological feature, it is smaller and less spectacular.

From the Fire Line

by Ed Brouwer, Fire Chief Canwest Fire,
Fire Warden MOF, "First ones in, last ones out!"

The year British Columbia burned is how 2003 will be remembered by most of us living in the west. Our hotshot crews "Sons of Thunder" and "Dragon Slayers," having just returned from the wildfire crisis in Osoyoos, B.C., were in the third day of our stand-by rotation when the call came. On August 16 at 11 a.m., Ministry of Forests (MOF) dispatched us to a lightning strike across from Antler Beach. Although an MOF Initial Attack crew, two helicopters and three CL 415 air tankers had been actioning the fire since early morning, the fire seemed to be gaining momentum. Unfortunately, a second fire broke out near Chute Lake and there were new flare-ups north of Kamloops, forcing authorities to divert air support before the noon hour.

The terrain we dealt with involved miles of canyons, valleys, and rock bluffs. Not only is it difficult to manoeuvre within these areas, they also have a direct influence on any wind flows in the area. Squally Point has the unique distinction of being a place where winds split. A portion flows north along the lake toward the City of Kelowna, the other portion flows south along the lake toward Naramata, often driving the fire in two directions at the same time. If that wasn't bad enough, Wild Horse Canyon, which cuts across Okanagan Mountain Park, has openings on both sides of Squally Point. This factor influenced winds flowing in both the Kelowna and Naramata directions forcing them into the canyon openings. This constriction caused the winds to gain speed and pressure (Funnel Effect). In short, we faced erratic gusting winds changing direction and force. Circular winds caused dust devils at times 100 metres in the air. We would discover later that the high winds caused spotting up to 3.2 kilometres ahead of the fire.

After landing on the beach, we climbed up the steep mountainside and hooked up with the Initial Attack crew. For several hours we dug hand guards and patrolled the fire perimeter. Retardant drops were being made to the north of us and water drops were being made on the flanks but were not as effective as we had hoped due to the depth of the duff. Because the duff layer was so dry and deep, the fire would burn right under the retardant and far too often make an escape. Turbulent winds lifted burning embers, setting them down across the guards.

The second day following the fire's edge, we climbed to the 1000 metre level and working with the Initial Attack crew, put in over three kilometres of hand guard. The third day found us at even higher altitudes and in rougher terrain. The smoke column hung ominously above us. The wind's changing directions caused fire whirls and blow-ups. All three days had brought unstable air masses and erratic fire behaviour but today was different. Sometimes you just get that feeling. Sure enough, by 16:00 hours we were warned that 70 kilometre per hour winds were predicted to push the fire back on top of us. We were to prepare for immediate helicopter evacuation. The 30 of us were flown to a staging area in Peachland where we awaited further orders.

The smoke column over the fire was now a huge mushrooming mass. The colour of the smoke indicated a very intense, hot fire. We never did go back to Squally Point. The high winds drove the fire over the guards with such intensity that it devoured our bladders, hose lines, and medivac kits. Over the next few days we would find out exactly just how vicious this fire dragon was going to be. In one day it grew from 2,000 hectares to more than 11,000. Firefighting conditions were the worst fire officials had ever seen. The Okanagan Mountain Park Fire became a wind driven, terrain agitated fire that would, in the end, attack Kelowna in the north and Naramata in the south. Our crews were moved to the Naramata side.

Fire crews worked tirelessly as the weekend approached. Thanks to the quick and decisive work of the South Division firefighters, Naramata was spared. Fortunately, all things worked in our favour when we did the back fire on the south side. Firefighters, skidders, and operators lined the guards put in by the D8-Cats. The signal was given and the chopper carrying the heli-torch made several passes dropping burning liquid fuel. The tinder dry forests between the guard and the fire ignited at an alarming rate. We had Rank 5 within minutes after ignition. There were several escapes, but by 1 a.m. we were able to contain them. Exhausted beyond description, we headed out to get a few hours of sleep. In far too short of a time we were back at it. But the threat to Naramata had been stayed.

More than once we were forced to use our escape routes running for safety. On one occasion we went back through the flames and smoke to get a couple of equipment operators out. We were cooled down by the "Ducks" and tankers as we ran for safety. Operators had to leave their heavy equipment to burn as they ran for their lives. Several firefighters were hospitalized after their $250,000 fire engine rolled down an embankment when the bank of the road gave way in Naramata. Thankfully, no lives were lost in this historic battle with the fire dragon.

Twice during the height of the crisis, the families of our crew were evacuated from their homes as the fire threatened the eastern outskirts of Kelowna. Other hotshot crews offered to help defend our homes and pilots offered to assist; however, we all knew the task at hand was much bigger than our personal places. Although the public referred to us as heroes, no one I met working the fire line thought themselves worthy of the "hero" title. We were simply answering the call.

The public's expressions of gratitude were overwhelming. The following two accounts stand out for our crew. We had just put in a 14 hour day on the Naramata side and we stopped for gas in Summerland. A young man sitting in a beat up old pick-up truck stared at the six of us dressed in our "reds" covered in black ash and a bone tired weariness. I saw him look at his two young children on the seat next to him. As though given the go ahead from them, he opened his door and approached us. As he came near he stretched out his hands and quietly said, "I wish I could do more, thank you so much." In his hands he held two peaches, two of the most beautiful peaches this world has ever seen. I looked past the young man and saw his two children quietly sitting, awaiting their father's return. A freak wind must have come up because a number of us got something in our eyes all at the same time. We spoke often of that simple, yet great act of appreciation.

Then there was the gray haired old man we passed every morning on the way to staging. The first day we saw him he was walking along the road to Naramata collecting bottles. He looked up when he heard us coming and when he saw that we were firefighters, he straightened up and stood at full attention, saluting us as we drove past. You sir, whoever you are, boosted our morale every day that week. Thank you so much.

As the fire threatened to run east towards Big White and Idabel Lake resort areas a "miracle rain" came at the midnight hour and forced the fire to burn back on itself. That was the turning point. From then on, it was only a matter of time. With the help of army and navy personnel we sought out as many hotspots as possible.

As our crew drove into Kelowna on our last day, the bone tired weariness that had haunted us for days was lifted by a renewed determination to actively pursue a provincial interface fire service. This year's reign of fire has proven the need for more cross training between wildland and structural firefighters and a greater understanding of what a "defensible space" is for those living in the interface.

Chapter Two
Getting Out

"I looked around my living room, said goodbye to grandfather's rocking chair, my most cherished belonging, sat down in it, and waited.
On our street everything was empty and, except for the sound of water sprinklers, quiet – very quiet. Never has the sight of my husband in our red Subaru seemed dearer."

MARIANNE PFISTER

"I heard a voice saying, 'Albert, start packing.' It was the voice of my wife. The next thing I knew, my obedient son-in-law, to his mother-in-law that is, started taking down the pictures from off the wall. A few of my books, a couple of shirts, two pairs of pants, extra pair of shoes, my wallet, passport and I was shipped to my daughter's home in Glenmore, a haven for evacuees."

ALBERT BALDEO

WHAT REALLY MATTERS?
BY ELIZABETH LYCAR

Walking out of my house the day I was **evacuated,** I knew I should be feeling something. I should be horrified, terrified, scared, stunned, bewildered, unprepared, something. But – I have the photograph to prove it – I was none of those things. In the picture I am smiling as I carried an object out of the house, rescuing it from the firestorm.

It was a cheap clay pot, spray-painted, containing artificial flowers and a candle. The centerpiece from my daughter's wedding. This was the first clue that I was actually in a state of surreal stupor. I was carrying on as though everything was normal. Sure, the sky was an eerie shade of dusty magenta – something I've never seen before, but this whole thing wasn't real to me. I did not expect that knock on the door and I never expected to have to leave my house on account of a fire that started a week earlier and seemed to be miles away. On the news the night before, I had been surprised when I saw a woman rescuing an infinitesimally small, spindly plant. "Why is she taking that?" I wondered. Why now was I taking a five-dollar centrepiece?

At the same time, my husband, who had earlier wandered from room to room saying there was nothing he needed to save, was now carting out the TV and my son was making helpful suggestions. "If you're going to take the TV, you may as well take the VCR, too."

We nodded and disconnected the wires. After all, we wouldn't want to be homeless without any entertainment. Then just as we made the final pass, the same husband started unplugging the phone and answering machine.

"Yes," I agreed, "we should take those." A lot of good an answering machine was going to do us unless it was plugged into our phone line, but we weren't paying attention to common sense right then.

We all got into different vehicles. We were rescuing a friend's motor home (which the day before had been filled with the genuinely important things – our cat and some photographs), so we had more vehicles than drivers. A decision was quickly made: the son's rusty Honda would have to be sacrificed. The back seat of my car had a TV, VCR, telephone and answering machine and the centrepiece from my daughter's wedding. Things we evidently could not live without. We each got into our assigned transportation. As if on some sort of cue, we simultaneously got out again and trooped back into the house. Something else had to be done – sweep the floor maybe? I never go on vacation without first giving the house a good cleaning.

When we unpacked our suitcases at our temporary accommodation, my son realized all he had put in his gym bag were three sweaters. This was not good. It was 35 degrees outside and an inferno was raging nearby. We would have to go shopping, so the next day we went to the mall. It is a strange feeling to be looking at material things when you don't know the status of your current belongings. You begin to detach from possessions altogether; so we wandered aimlessly, fingering this and that, and buying nothing.

At a time like this, you realize all that really matters are the people, the pets and maybe, just maybe, the centrepiece from your daughter's wedding.

A Little Help From My Friends

by Martha Neumann

I'm a senior, past 65, retired, and I live alone in Kettle Valley, Kelowna.

My story actually begins in July 2003. That's when I moved into my house. I hadn't had a chance to settle down and still had a lot of boxes to unpack when the Okanagan Mountain Park Fire started. At first I wasn't worried at all and never believed that our neighbourhood would be evacuated, (nobody did), even after we were placed on alert status. I still believed the fire would turn away from us.

Then came Thursday, August 21. Within minutes in the late afternoon, the air was so full of smoke that it got completely dark like the night. I ran outside but could hardly see anything. Only a huge, big fire all around our neighbourhood, which was now clearly out of control and was moving very rapidly toward Kettle Valley. I knew then that it was time to leave.

I went into the garage, opened all four doors of my car and the trunk, and started filling up the car with some of my belongings. I took my time, running back and forth for approximately 25 to 30 minutes. It was now about 7:30 or 8 p.m. and I noticed that, in the meantime, almost everybody had left. I was the last one still there. Quickly, I locked the doors, jumped into my car and turned the ignition key – and I froze – absolutely nothing happened, not a sound – the car was dead. I tried again and again – nothing. The battery was dead. All my neighbours were gone, nobody there to call for help. Fear and panic grabbed me. The fire was close and it looked spooky. I ran back into the house to call 911. I explained to the operator (I believe her name was Carrie) what had happened to me, and naturally I sounded desperate. She was very nice, tried to calm me down and asked me not to hang up the phone. She would notify the police and then get back to me. While I was still waiting on the phone, all the lights suddenly went out and the phone went dead. A power failure due to the fire.

I'm not too easily scared, but I was frightened and scared now. I was all alone in the dark, with all connections cut off and all neighbours gone. The huge fire was creeping closer. Helicopters were flying over my house. My next step was to find a candle and light it, which I did with shaking hands. And then, after a few minutes, the power came back on again and the telephone started ringing. It was my friend Helen H., who was concerned about me, wondering why I hadn't left yet. I explained my desperate situation. She said she would talk to her son Richard right away and see if he could help me. Then I called 911 again. Carrie recognized me right away and said the police were on their way to my house. (I had given her my name and address just before the phone went dead). The bad news was, she said, that the police had no battery cables and would not be able to start my car. But they would, of course, pick me up and get me to the registration centre. Dear Lord, I thought, now I am going to lose everything, even the car and the few things in it. I just cried.

I went back into the garage to give it one more try – no luck. While I was in the garage, a truck stopped in front of me. It was Richard, Helen's son. He started working on my car right away. What a relief – what good friends!

Meanwhile, two or three police cars also arrived in front of my house. One young man rushed into the garage to help Richard. A nice police woman talked to me, tried to calm me down. Then, the men came in and announced that the car was running. That was wonderful news. I thanked everybody wholeheartedly, locked the doors (again) and off I went.

On my way to K.S.S. on Raymer Avenue, while I was driving down Chute Lake Road ever so slowly due to the volume of traffic, I kept thinking that all my treasured possessions, like my beautiful antique desk, the piano, grandfather clock, paintings, etc., were probably devoured now by those horrible flames. And the tears kept running down my face.

At the registration centre, everybody was very friendly, well organized, efficient, and helpful. I was given a nice room in the Holiday Inn. Two days later my good and dear friend Frank V., who knew about my predicament, came down to the hotel with a brand new car battery. In no time at all he had it installed and refused to take any money. Thanks again, Frank, from the bottom of my heart. Also many thanks to all the others who were so helpful and supportive during this time of great stress. It really has been appreciated.

Not knowing if I really lost everything or not was pure agony. Then, I found out I was one of the lucky ones and that my house and all the others on our street were saved. It's hard to describe my joy and happiness after receiving this good news. At the same time, my sincerest sympathy goes out to the families who were not so lucky and lost all their possessions. How close I had come!

Soon we were allowed to return to our homes. Aside from a strong smoke odour inside and outside the house, and some spoiled food in the freezer, everything else was fine.

I will never forget the night when my car gave up just when I needed it the most. But my life is pretty well back to normal again and I appreciate everything around me and everything I have.

Sometimes I feel a little lonely but in general I feel very lucky, very grateful, and very blessed.

One Last Pot
by June Bevan

It was late afternoon, Friday August 22, 2003. My husband and our son-in-law Errol were barbecuing outdoors while our daughter and I prepared food in the kitchen. The evening before, we had received a call from her in the Upper Mission. "Can you come and help us get out? Errol is away with the van, and I need help. We've got to leave right away!"

We had fast-tracked from our home in Ellison as far as Dehart and Lakeshore roads before running into a roadblock. Dozens of vehicles were moving north. We were soon queried as to our intent then allowed to pass in the interest of helping family. Two more roadblocks intensified our distress and it was evident by a red glow in the sky that the situation was serious. Tension in the air was almost palpable.

We reached Joyce and Errol's home to find them frantically hauling stuff out and packing their vehicles, Errol and the van having arrived home. Much later, with many belongings stowed elsewhere, our very small retirement home was solidly peopled with three extra adults and two teenagers. Now, less than twenty-four hours later, we were all to be on the move again.

The upper Mission area had been on alert for several days and knowing that our kids were on alert, I began a list of things I would take and had readied a few boxes and bins, just in case.

Dinner Friday evening was tense: tracking TV newscasts, frequent gazing in a southerly direction. Joyce became more concerned as the sky took on a redder hue. "That's just the way it looked last night. The fire's coming this way!" It did appear to be so, but for the moment we were safe.

And then the dreaded announcement on TV: Ellison has to evacuate. Panic gripped me. Two hours to pack up a lifetime. How does one do that? With much confusion, I was to learn. Uncertainty and indecision were followed by quick judgments and a great feeling of nostalgia for what had to be left behind.

Then everybody seemed to move at once, hauling out bags and boxes that were packed, hastily gathering up what was at hand. Being of an orderly bent, I headed for the kitchen to wash dishes. I was almost finished before logic took over. "You silly woman," I said to myself, "your house might burn down, but at least the kitchen will be tidy," whereupon I turned the last pot into the sink and joined in the packing frenzy.

It would be impossible for our grandson to take his aquarium tanks. He sat beside them in the living room, seemingly oblivious to the activity around him, distressed, and wondering if his beloved creatures would survive.

I was determined to take as much stuff as we could "stuff" into the van, and emptied closets and cupboards as long as time allowed. Someone turned out the contents of bathroom shelves and later I discovered a garbage bag half full of toilet tissue among the stuff. Well, at least we had that!

All too soon, the call to leave came. A resigned farewell glance at what we were leaving, a quick check to ask if neighbours needed help, then we were away. I wondered if we would ever see our little house again. Even so, there was a degree of relief knowing we were escaping danger.

We did see our home again when, two days later, we were allowed to return. And there was the pot from Friday's dinner, still soaking in the sink.

After the evacuation I decided that next time, I'd call a moving truck right away and clean out the house. In retrospect, however, I think my response would be different. We do become attached to things for various reasons, and emotion can take over. While I would be sorry to lose things I treasure, they are, after all, only things and I believe I could let go more easily now. Someone said a long time ago that life does not consist of the abundance of things one possesses. I know that, after the crisis of 2003, many in the city would concur.

AN EXCERPT FROM

THE FIRE by Sharon Thesen

I want the house clean

for the fire; to the greater

scourging, I offer the lesser.

Windex, the floor mop, the

sink stopper polished with Vim,

the whole nine yards,

the whole ball of wax.

Last week we'd twirled

Mars to clarity inside

binoculars, made several

observations: its proximity,

its redness, the likelihood

of life.

And this morning

the vacuum cleaner is travelling

along behind. I apologize

to a pillow, I can't take you,

dear, like throwing a maiden

off a cliff, well, not quite,

but the sense of propitiation

was there: Fire, here is a clean floor.

Fire, here is an innocent cushion

Not Just Another Headline

by Glenna Turnbull

To many in the world, the Okanagan Mountain Park Fire was just another headline, just another tragedy happening to someone else, somewhere else; something to shake their head about and say, "how sad" in between bites of their morning bagel. But to those of us who live here, it's an experience that branded its imprint on us for life.

Fire is a natural part of the Okanagan ecosystem. Just like the hot dry summers and far too cloudy winters, fire is part of the cycle that makes our valley unique. But in our usual "human can conquer all" way of thinking, we assumed we could cheat Mother Nature out of housecleaning the forests around our residential neighbourhoods. Apparently, we were wrong.

But as devastating as the fire was, as we start sifting through the ashes, a rainbow of stories began to appear.

My own story started at the Salmon Arm Roots and Blues Festival. We'd been listening to CBC radio as we drove to Salmon Arm, hearing interviews with people from Barrier who had lost their homes. Like the headline, "Hurricane Devastates the East Coast," Barrier seemed a long way away, and I nodded and said, "how sad." The following day, however, as ashes started to rain down on the festival from the nearby Chase fire, it seemed a little more real, but still, it was something happening to someone else.

Driving back from the festival, we learned of the lightning strike that hit Okanagan Mountain Park while we were away and as we got closer to Kelowna, we could see the huge plume of smoke rising and suddenly, it no longer seemed like someone else's headline. This was real.

In the days that followed, ashes began tumbling from the sky, leaving a very surreal landscape under an ominous orange sun. The smoke in the air made everything look like we were in some movie from the 1950s. Leaves, still perfectly shaped but carbonized, were landing on the lawn; pine needles charred but recognizable; a piece of tar paper the size of a business card floated down into the yard, "probably part of someone's house," my boyfriend Kelly said. On the hood of my truck, it looked like dirty snow.

We left for Big White on Friday afternoon before the winds. We had our names on lists to volunteer and couldn't do anything more here, so we decided to get out of the smoke. At that point, although our friends Ron and Lydia had already lost their home on Timberline, the fire seemed to be staying contained within the new firewalls built by the city and we thought the worst was over.

We arrived at the cabin to clear air, the smell of pine and quiet. Living close to the Apple Bowl, the army had been stationed 300 metres from my door and the sound of their helicopters flying in and out at all hours had been overwhelming. The quiet on the mountain was like being able to just shut the door on all the madness. But as soon as we turned on the cabin radio, we realized the madness was inescapable. The fire had gone completely out of control again, evacuations now affected one third of our town and Hwy 33, the road out of Big White back to Kelowna, was closed.

Saturday morning we awoke to the news that up to 200 homes may have been lost and we spent the day listening to the radio for any updates we could get as to which direction the fire was moving. We heard statistics of the fire's speed, said to be moving at rates between 100 and 200 metres per minute. Not knowing where the head of the fire was, combined with the thick smoke that started blowing into Big White, had me feeling edgy. "It comes in waves," my friend John Mooney, a volunteer firefighter at Big White told me as the smoke continued to creep in. "Don't worry, we're safe here."

John was back at our door a few hours later to tell us about an information meeting for all Big White residents, starting in 10 minutes. When we got there, the fire chief told us we were officially on an evacuation alert. They said they would endeavour to give us a two-hour notice but that they couldn't promise anything. We all had to register as being on the mountain and were given a meeting place to convoy out from if our evacuation became necessary.

That's when the reality of the fire really hit. Kelly and I went back to the cabin and I started unpacking the laundry crates, wanting to know we'd have somewhere to put things if we needed them. I began looking around at all the things so cherished, thinking of all the families who had gone through their homes in the past few days, picking out what they would take, what they couldn't afford to lose.

Looking around, I asked, what is important? What really, really matters when you're faced with the thought of having your house burn down? To my son's friend Naomi, who was evacuated and moved into our house in Kelowna, it was her cat, her computer, a suitcase full of clothes, a bag of shoes, her graduation dress and photographs. My lawyer, on the other hand, was trying to find an enclosed garage to store his antique Jaguar. What would I save?

All of these emotions compounded upon each other and I found myself turning more and more to Kelly, so thankful to have him with me, like some kind of silly reassurance that having a man beside me would keep me safe. We turned the radio off for an hour or two at a time and put on a CD, allowing ourselves an escape from the intensity of the news to find comfort in each other. Everything we did became sacred. I even blurted out that I wished we were married.

We woke up Sunday morning to calm winds and Hwy 33 re-opened back into Kelowna, but Kelly decided he did not want to leave in case they did evacuate and he couldn't get back up to get our things. I had no choice but to get back while I could, and as I drove along Hwy 33 passed a convoy of some 30 or more fire trucks from places like Chemainus, Salt Spring and other far away places, all heading to Mission Creek to fill up, that's when I finally lost it. As I beeped my horn, waving and yelling thank you to all the firefighters who saw this fire as more than just a headline of news happening somewhere else, I burst into tears and let them shamelessly flow down my face, thankful there were no reporters around to capture the image of an overwhelmed woman balling her eyes out, something for tomorrow's front page.

Under Alien Sun

by Gord Grisenthwaite

The air was thick with foreshadowing, a cross between the sophisticated, quiet terror of Alfred Hitchcock's work and the cheesy, over the top sort of daytime television. It was thick with other stuff, too. For about eleven days, breathing had been a chore; more than once I seriously considered admitting myself into the hospital.

The valley was under a thick, grey-black smoke tent that muffled sound, cast ash like snow flurries, and painted the sun alien red-orange. We watched the sky, the horizon, and constantly looked over our shoulders each time we stepped outside. As the fire burned nearer the city, licked up neighbourhoods in the Mission, as more and more families were placed on alert or evacuated, we convinced ourselves that the fire couldn't touch us, not on Black Mountain. They overreacted. Their reports were sensationalized. When the fire's licking at my doorstep, I'll act, I thought. After all, I had been through devastating forest fires before, fires that burned far closer to Lytton, my childhood home.

Do you put your life on hold and wait on the whim of fire and wind, or do you carry on as best you can? We chose to carry on. It was Friday, the night my nephews and I played cards at Quantum Games. We expected a low turnout, but the store was packed. A few parents picked up their kids before the tournament started. Many made jokes about which of Quantum's inventory we would rescue from the flames, if it came to that. In the background, the radio droned news of the fire's advances. The evacuation line approached and then passed the store. By eight o'clock, Al, the store's owner, asked everyone who was not competing to leave. My nephews and I left. I looked south along Hollywood and for the first time since the fire started, panic welled up inside me.

"Let's get home," I said, "before the roadblocks go up." We mounted our bikes and rode toward Highway 33. Traffic flowed steadily in all four directions. Riding our bikes along Highway 33 was like riding in a WWII movie: the exodus prior to German occupation. All that was missing was the sound of the air raid sirens. The only noise was the drone of the traffic. There were no boom boxes, no conversations. The air was thick with panic, with grim fear.

Around Prior Avenue, my brother, heading west, flagged us down and shouted instructions. His words were swallowed by the traffic noise. He continued to the rendezvous. We didn't know where it was, but between the three of us we decided that he said South Rutland Elementary. Some twenty minutes later we found the school. We found it dark, desolate. It was not one of the places set up to register evacuees. We headed to Rutland Secondary School, thinking that was where we were to rally and to register. From there we went to Parkinson Recreation Centre.

We registered. There was no sign of my brother. The boys were worried that he was safe. They were near tears. I choked back fear and tears through the process and with the help of some awesome volunteers, convinced the boys that their dad would find us.

We were dispatched to Skyreach Place. We got there a little after eleven o'clock. None of us had eaten since early afternoon. We parked our bikes and went straight to the concession. The menu was a buzz of jumbled letters. My stomach growled. Internally, I was building a to do list: leave a message for the boys' father; get the boys settled, fed, and ready for bed; get Pat replacement meds;

get us toothbrushes and toothpaste; and make a list of essential clothing—we had only that which we wore.

I was thirsty. I needed to eat. I was decisioned out. The boys wanted to order, kept asking me if it was okay if they had a pop, some fries, a hot dog, and a hamburger. They were only ten feet from me but I felt they were too far from me. I moved closer to them like a fussy mother hen. I hoped that my fear was masked by my casual manner. As I passed the check-in table, I heard a man repeat his name, and ask why there were no evacuees assigned to his billet: he'd registered days ago.

"Well, then" he said at last, "I guess I'll just grab the next two that walk through those doors." Even though we were three, it turns out that he meant us. His name was Bill Nimmo.

He and his family welcomed us into their home. I was numb. I was clear about what I needed to do and clear about relaying the needs in order. Bill drove us to the pharmacy to get Pat's meds, to Zeller's, and once there he took Pat and helped him select his clothing. I guided Trevor and shopped for myself. Bill fixed Trevor's bike. The family treated us like honoured guests. They helped us reconnect with the boys' father. They were awesome. I was numb.

After nearly three days, the boys were reunited with their father. I snuck past the roadblock to tend to the animals and property. I watched the news as I hadn't since Desert Storm. I watched the hills under the alien sun. I rested little until the evacuation order was lifted on August 27. It's taken some time, but I realize now that the fire had a harsher effect on me than I've so far admitted: that life under the alien sun was far from normal and average.

The Lost Address Book
by Asia Sayr Ladd

Friday afternoon I was having coffee with the owner of a gift shop and the only topic of discussion was the fire and its progress. I wasn't concerned. She was. She told me, "You should go home right now and start packing your valuables."

I easily packed my personal mementos and, as I do not have insurance, loaded my computer too. I have a motor scooter and one of the apple pickers in the orchard where I live hoisted it into his van and stored it in one of my landlord's large sheds. It occurred to me that the scooter may not make it through the fire but I tried not to focus on that. I stored my car's contents at a friend's garage then returned home.

Early in the morning my cat had taken off and didn't come home. My dog knew something was wrong. I leashed her up so I'd be able to get her when we needed to go. I had the luxury of three hours notice to pack my original contents and then time for another load.

I felt very calm, peaceful almost. I didn't have insurance, but I knew my landlord did. If the fire came he would rebuild and I was sure that would include building a little cabin again. It was summer and I had a teepee so, except for the left-over contents of my cabin, I would survive rather easily. Around 4 p.m. the fire had crested the hill towards our cabins.

The odd thing about fires getting so close is that all you can see is red and black and all you hear is the sucking sound of the dragon devouring air – our air, all the air. It was time to leave. Now! My dog and I were put up at a dear friend's home and then, like the other evacuees, I went to register. We expected to wait but to our surprise the line moved swiftly, almost in pace with the fire. From then on, I was captivated by the news and had the radio on for days and days on end, giving us minute to minute coverage and keeping the phone lines open for people to express themselves. Off air staff also worked tirelessly to give information to people who needed it.

The next day I went to Orchard Plaza to get my eyeglasses fixed as they had managed to get out of shape during the last day or so. I took my dog with me as she was much too unsettled to be left alone. My car, still packed with the second load of belongings, was broken into. I had left two windows down a bit for my dog to breathe. Someone took my briefcase which had my Lions roster, my personal address book and an envelope with all my savings ($600) inside. After I realized what had happened, I tried to make a police report but they were swamped and told me it would be Monday before I could report the theft.

Being retired and disabled, the monetary loss was hard to take. Losing my address book hit me right in the gut. There were names and information I would never be able to recover. I mourned the loss of an address book and felt guilty for doing so when so many others lost so much more, went through so much more. There were hundreds of families without homes and mementos. There were firemen who faced the dragon and gulped down their own fears and nightmares.

In the end my house was still there. My cat came home unscathed and the Salvation Army helped me monetarily. Today I volunteer for the Salvation Army. Also I am putting together the Phoenix Exhibit, a travelling display of the fire memorabilia. And as far as my address book – it was the last thing in the last box that I unpacked when I was sure it was safe to be home. There is a God. For me it was finding an address book; for others, especially the frontline firefighters (including those who lost homes), it was that no one died.

What Should One Take?
by Sharon Shepherd

It was in our friends' home in Lake Country, after being evacuated a second time from my parents' home in lower Mission, that I saw the Christmas decoration in the corner. "Oh my goodness," I cried. I realized we hadn't packed any of our Christmas decorations, including the stockings I'd made that we've had for so many years. Tears poured down my face.

Very late the previous evening, the fire had raged right through our neighbourhood. Our home has cedar shakes, cedar siding and there are large ponderosa pines right in the decks near the front and back doors. We were sure our home was gone.

A call only a few hours later from a friend who had tracked us down gave us hope. "I was looking through binoculars from here on the Westside and I am sure I can see our home and yours, but it looks quite bad above us and there is still lots of fire and smoke," he excitedly stated. My husband and I hugged each other and could hardly wait to head to a place where we might be able to see our area.

For days at Gyro beach, many of us sat and watched the smoke and continual fleet of aircraft dropping water on the south slopes. Using binoculars, we thought we could see the trees still surrounding our home. We thought that was a good sign!

When we were finally allowed back home, the smoke in the air was heavy and lingered inside the house as well. It wasn't until the next morning that we saw the burnt portion of property outside our kitchen window. Apparently, the helicopters dropping water along our street and the sudden change in wind saved the homes on the lower part of Viewcrest.

As we moved our possessions back home, we looked around and recognized what we hadn't taken. In addition to the Christmas decorations, we'd also forgotten our address book, some of the special wines in our wine cellar, and our special cookbooks and recipes that we'd saved over the years.

We have started to do a cleaning of our home along with an inventory of our accumulations from more than 32 years of marriage. I began discovering things we had forgotten about. We repainted some walls and hung many of our pictures in different places. Our home feels somewhat different than it did before we evacuated last August.

If we ever have to evacuate again, we would do things differently. We would only take those things that cannot be replaced, whether because of monetary or sentimental value. We still need to finish the video and inventory of our contents. Just imagine if you only had a few minutes, a few hours, or a few days and had to leave your home. How prepared would you be?

I have still not quite completed my list of preparedness. But that's okay, my husband says we are now living in the safest area around!

Chapter Three
Helping Hands

"We must be thankful for the community spirit here in the Okanagan which is so amazing in so many ways."

SANDRA ANNE KESSLER

"All my friends had either vacated or were on call. Such a lonely, desolate feeling I'd never experienced before in my 82 years of living...
We all in our church gave new blankets, pillows, etc., but this is what really made me believe in humanity: Sitting on the verandah with my cat, the fire was burning trestles so close, making a terrible noise. So as not to be alone and frightened, I went reluctantly to the group next door, wondering should I or shouldn't I, as they're as young as my grandchildren. I stood near a young man who said, "Don't worry Grandma, we'd never let anything happen to you or your cat."

ANNE SMITHANIK

WE ALL LOVE GIRL GUIDE COOKIES

BY CAPTAIN TED VIZZUTTI

I am a Career Captain with Powell River **Fire Rescue** and have been with the department for the past **18 years.** On September 4, 2003 Director of Emergency Services, D. Gerhart, asked if I would like to travel to Kelowna and participate in fighting the wild land fires. This would be the third group from Powell River to travel to Kelowna to help.

The journey began on September 5, 2003 at approximately 0630 hrs. at which time Director Gerhart, myself, and five auxiliary firefighters left with Engine 1 and a support vehicle. The trip lasted approximately 12 hours and our travels brought us past Okanagan Lake and the point of origin for this devastating fire. Upon arrival at Kelowna Fire Station #1, we were one group of many firefighters that came to help. Thank you letters were posted all over the hall. What a feeling. We were advised our crew would be assigned to a gel team and to report at 0800 hrs on September 6, 2003. From the hall and our hotel we could see the fires burning. What a sight.

We were staying at one of the local hotels and this is where I first encountered how the fires were affecting Kelowna residents. On both sides of my room were families that had evacuated their homes. On one side was an elderly gentleman and his wife, and he stated that he expected his home to burn that night and that his life would change. He was more than appreciative that firefighters from other communities would come to Kelowna and help. On the other side was a young family with children who also had to leave their home and live in a small hotel room. One of the children, a young boy, had come down with the flu and was not well. As I was talking to the father, the boy came out and he was really under the weather, so I asked the father if the boy would like to see the fire truck. Instantly, a change in the boy could be noticed but this surge of energy would not last. As he was sitting in the driver's seat the colour disappeared from his face and his energy diminished. That was as much as he could stand, back to the strange room he went.

All I could imagine was, here is a sick young boy in a strange place, strange room and all he wanted was his own bed in his familiar home and room with all his toys but that was not happening. I thought about how my family would react.

The next day we started our job and for the next 28 hours we would train, preplan the area and prepare on how to use the gel product and protect the homes. After a full night of being on alert, ready and watching the fire high above us on the mountain ridges, we received the orders to stand down at noon but were on alert as the winds were picking up again. Sure enough we were called back in that evening; our assignment was to go up into the Gallagher's Canyon area and gel the homes just below the new advancing fire line. The Powell River crew along with Mad Burn Gel Company headed up into the bushes on a dirt road towards a small subdivision of homes.

Upon arrival at the first home we were met with a small problem. The owners had evacuated but for some reason unknown to us they had decided to leave the family dog behind and tied to the home. It was a friendly black lab but was obviously scared and if the fires had reached their home, the dog would not have made it. A decision was made between Chief Gerhart and I that the dog could not stay and that we would bring it out with us. The dog was placed into the back seat of the chief's vehicle and was given some water and Girl Guide cookies that I had with me in the fire truck. The dog was nervous but after a bit, he ate them. For the next hour the dog rode with us as we gelled the homes. I felt that taking the dog with us was saving him and allowing the family to have their dog once again.

We drove back to Fire Hall #7 after our job was completed and from there we contacted the S.P.C.A. The dog was taken and the family was to be notified that their friend was safe.

This is a memory that I will remember and

is one of the reasons why I do this job.

Girl Guides Lend a Hand

by Lynn Waller, Provincial Product Marketing Adviser
Girl Guide Cookies, BC Girl Guides

The upheaval of evacuating your house on a half hour notice and the sounds of three or four helicopters nearby with the help of water bombers are not a normal part of daily activities. Neither is having smoke so heavy in the air that your eyes burn, or seeing ash flying through the air along with burnt leaves and twigs. But this was the reality for the City of Kelowna in August 2003. The day of the firestorm, an appeal went out for volunteers to assist in the two evacuation centres in the city.

Adult members in Guiding and girls of many levels in Girl Guides outdid themselves in their volunteering. In a matter of hours, Girl Guides loaded cookies and dropped them off and Guiding members were on hand in the evacuation centres assisting – quite an emotional task. Each volunteer and evacuated family was given a box of cookies. Cookies were also taken to the main Kelowna fire hall where the girls were greeted with many smiles, tears, and hugs. The RCMP and the BC Ambulance personnel also received cases of cookies in recognition of their important and vital roles during the Okanagan Mountain Fire.

One evening, visits were made by Guiders to the BC Forestry fire camp on the west side of Okanagan Lake where the forestry firefighters were staying. Cookies were placed at all the tents and on some sleeping bags before the majority of the hardworking men and women came back from another tough day on the fire lines. When they arrived, the firefighters were very appreciative of the Girl Guides and the gesture of support in their effort.

Another evening, a visit was made to the military camp set up at the Apple Bowl, Kelowna's home field to the Okanagan Sun football team. This military camp looked like something out of M*A*S*H with the huge army and navy trucks, tents, and military police. When our vans pulled up and we said, "Girl Guide cookies?" they led us right into the camp. The conversations were interesting and inspiring. After talking with many from the Edmonton army, we are quite sure sales in Alberta for Girl Guide cookies will have a special increase in future campaigns.

A special afternoon was planned by the Central Okanagan Girl Guides at Trinity Baptist Church where evacuated families could drop off their children for an afternoon of games and crafts. Several Guiders showed up to assist along with members from Scouts Canada, which were also affected as the fire damaged their Mission area camp, Camp Dunlop.

Cookies were also given out to several heavy equipment operators. Word has it that many cookies made it to the fire trucks, going up to fight the massive fire.

Walk a Mile in My Shoes

by Marcia Goodwin, R.N.,B.Sc.N

As I was driving over the Okanagan Lake bridge early one August morning, I noticed a large column of smoke billowing out from behind Okanagan Mountain near Kelowna. The moment I turned on the radio, I heard that lightning had struck a tree and started a fire in the mountain park. With dismay, I realized I had hiked there just a few months ago. That hike, although comical at the time, became a treasured experience.

At 8:30 a.m. sharp that day in May, I met up with a group of hikers from the Kelowna Naturalists Club. It was easy to spot them: they were the ones in khaki pants, fleece vests and floppy hats who stood in well worn hiking boots looking very physically fit. Most of them had either white or grey hair with cheerful, wise, wrinkled faces. They chatted merrily amongst themselves and ever so politely critiqued my sneakers.

Without a word, just a warm smile and a friendly nod, they started to climb...straight up... and I began to zigzag! Before long I could hear my heart pounding so loud I thought they could hear it too. "Don't worry dear, you can make it," called a cheerful voice over her shoulder, "after all, if we can do it, so can you..."
"...Although if you zigzag, you'll go twice as far," chuckled another.

We continued to climb for the next hour. I didn't realize how out of shape I was and the terrain was very difficult. The ground was dry and sandy from drought, causing each footstep to slide down. There were no green shrubs to grab onto and the dry, spiralled ponderosa pine needles, which were piled a few feet thick in some places were slippery underfoot. I also had to avoid slipping on the tightly closed pinecones scattered all over the ground.

Evidence of the drought was everywhere. Ponds were so dried up some had no water at all. All that was left were the dry, exposed rocks. We climbed for several hours – these seniors never stopped! Sometimes the slope was so steep, we crawled on all fours over piles of dry, decayed wood. At one point, an elderly gentleman offered me his hiking poles and after I learned not to skewer my neighbour or myself, I found them useful.

As we rounded the top of a mountain rim, we came to a rock outcrop and stopped for lunch. The view from our dining area was breathtaking. You could see up and down the Okanagan Valley right over the lake. Distant mountains were purple-blue and the wind made beautiful swirl patterns on the lake far below. As we munched on trail mix and rice cakes, we spotted mountain goats perched on the ledge below us! We found their bedding areas on the ledges of the lower cliffs. Tufts of goat hair as soft as duck down were found wedged between rocks and caught on the dried rock lichens.

That's when I learned the descent of a mountain is far harder on the body than the ascent. I thought they were joking, but they weren't! I don't know who was more relieved that I made it safely from the mountain that day but the experience proved to be a valuable one, personally and in other ways. I know the rugged terrain and ground conditions that our firefighters had to negotiate when they fought what became a fierce firestorm. It also inspired me to help the firefighters in a unique way.

58

As the local foot nurse, I voluntarily provided foot care at the local fire camp here in Westbank. As I worked on their feet, these young people talked about their experiences and I understood what they were talking about. They came off the mountain covered in soot from head to toe. Some were so exhausted, they fell asleep sitting at the table in the meal tent. They described the frustration of fighting a fire on an uphill slope surrounded by dry forest that constantly fed the flames and I remembered the dry pine needles. Some had blisters on top of blisters; some described feeling like their feet were on fire after running on the hot rock outcrops and smoking forest floor. Soles of boots melted. Heat that intense creates its own wind, they said, and at times the fire suddenly boiled forward moving and sounding like a roaring train. All they could do then was run out of its way. The sudden, intense heat made trees explode and hurled wood chunks hundreds of feet in the air. And then there were the fire holes; places where the fire was burning three feet beneath the forest surface. Unknowingly stepping through a fire hole could cause a boot to spontaneously burst into flame.

Some called them heroes but the ones I met told me they were just doing what they were trained to do. It was their job. They just happened to be good at what they did and gave it their best.

The Naturalists tell me the fire heat was so intense that the pine cones we saw scattered on the forest floor would have opened. They will be watching for the colours of the first flowers to grow in the burn area. I've also been told that mountain goats are the first animals to return to their home. They travel miles just to look at what has happened and return repeatedly until there is once again enough vegetation to support them.

I feel privileged to have walked through a forest in that phase of its life cycle. Forests are constantly growing, dying, and renewing themselves. Fortunately, I personally witnessed it all. This walk taught me about inner strength and perseverance, gave me greater appreciation of the delicate balances and harmonies within nature, and taught me how fragile and vulnerable life truly is. Who would have thought there was so much to learn from a simple walk through the woods?

Westbank Volunteers

by Jim and Linda MacDonald

My wife and I moved to Westbank four years ago. Our children are grown and have moved away from home. We have often talked about getting involved in the community but did not know with what.

We watched the fire grow from the start and travel up into the hills. We watched in disbelief, not knowing the devastation this monster was going to unleash. We watched in awe from our side of the lake as our dedicated firefighters fought to save the large white house and the houses in the Timberline area – saving some, but to no avail, losing some as well. My wife and I were still torn as to what to do. We had to do something.

Friday, I came home from work, got my wife and we took our dog for a walk to the dog beach. I was not ready for what I was about to see. The wind had come up to about 70 kilometres per hour and there was a huge wall of fire consuming everything in its path.

Through my binoculars, I could see our firefighters trying to save these homes. I was amazed. We will never forget what we witnessed that night. We went home and sat there, stunned. We couldn't believe what we had just seen.

The next morning, when we awoke, we knew we had to do something so we phoned the Parkinson Rec. Centre and talked to Emergency Social Services and asked if we could help in any way. They said to come down, that they could use all the help they could get.

That was the beginning of our involvement with the fire. My wife and I both work full time, so we would work during the day then go to the Rec. Centre until midnight each night until it was over. We met a lot of wonderful, caring people devoting a lot of time, doing whatever they could to help. We also met a lot of very strong and brave people, some who had lost everything but still found the will to smile at the people who were trying to help them.

In those few weeks, my wife and I witnessed a community and a city come together in a wonderful bond of people helping people that we had never seen before. We are so very, very proud to be members of this community and we will never forget the people we met.

We are now full time members of the E.S.S. of Kelowna and are very proud to be working with such very special and dedicated people like Beryl Itani.

Volunteer – What a Lovely Name!

by Sharon Boissonneault, Girl Guides
of Canada District Commissioner, Cooinda District

I am standing in a gymnasium of a brand new school, there are people everywhere, some have a panicked look on their faces, others are crying. It's a city in crisis. I'm here to help wherever they need me. I follow the crowd in, and find the volunteer table. We sign in, get a quick lesson on how things are being done, and then are asked to start our six hour shift or to come back later in the day and work until midnight. It's a 24 hour a day operation here. My shift starts at 6 p.m. and goes until midnight. I watch people come and go, some of whom I know. I go over, trying to be brave with a smile on my face, in a concerned way. The tears start to flow as they tell me the horror taking place in their neighbourhood. We hug and talk. I offer them any bit of comfort I can.

We are very busy, the town is burning and homes are being evacuated by the thousands. The lines are long and people are there, standing, too numb to think. We offer coffee, water, juice, something to eat, a hug. I see a girl with her mom. She is frightened and wearing what looks like a WWII face mask because she is having problems breathing from the smoke. I go over with a smile and ask if there is anything I could get them or do for them. They smile and decline my offer. I know where a box of Telus bears are, special Teddy bears for kids in crisis. I go out and get one for her. I tell her to hug him tight as he is frightened by the fire.

At midnight we are done our shift. There are still lots of people who need our help but the night crew has arrived. We pick up our belongings and leave to go home. Home! What a wonderful place, a safe place, a place where we can laugh and cry and just be ourselves. I am thinking of all the sad people I have talked to, have hugged and cried with tonight, and I know tomorrow when I go back it will start all over again. I am just one person and hopefully I have made a difference in others' lives when their world was crumbling all around them. I have met some wonderful people in the past seven days, people that have touched my life in a way I will never forget. I have worked side by side with people that, just like me, tried to make a difference.

I know now why I like the sound of "volunteer."

NO HUMAN LIFE WAS LOST BY R.L. DIEBOLT

When fire burned our valley
No human life was lost
Sparks, then smoke, flames and ash
Created mounting costs

Cost was not considered
Self-giving bore no price
The volunteers were endless
Their arms stretched out in might

Should I attempt to name them
Too many would I miss
We wept and prayed, shared and gave
Then came the end of it!

Foul smoke and eeriness
The sirens day and night
Are now replaced with cobalt skies
We see a heavenly sight

Somehow I know we're better
A family not apart
We share a hope born out of love
And know how great Thou art.

Thank God, no human life was lost.

The Hungarian Angel

by Cyril Chalk, Fire Recovery Coordinator, Kelowna Community Church of the Salvation Army

During the Okanagan Mountain Park Fire, so many people were involved in both fighting the fire and assisting the community. These reflections are a composite look composed from the recollections of several volunteers from The Salvation Army.

In the event of a major incident, the Provincial government's Emergency Social Service goes into action to assist victims of "disasters." Within the ESS protocol, provisions are made for many different agencies and community service groups to bring their talents and abilities together to assist the community. The Salvation Army has been assigned the specific task of "Meeting and Greeting" people who come to the reception centres and providing them with assistance there, whether that be direction, counselling, or whatever.

When the first evacuations occurred, a few of our folks reported directly to the Parkinson Recreation Centre to man the doors. Wednesday night's evacuation, while traumatic for the city's most southern residents, was small enough and slow enough that people volunteering had time to practice and prepare. The night passed quietly and we were able to get some rest and sleep, unaware that the next 48 hours would make tremendous demands on our community.

When the evacuation order came on Thursday evening, the number of people who were ordered to leave their homes surprised everyone. Several of our people had gone home and phone calls went out to get as many of our volunteers to Parkinson Rec Centre and, now, K.S.S. as well. People willingly rushed back to the sites, manned their posts, and were prepared to help because we realized the people who were leaving their homes were not strangers or statistics, they were our neighbours. As the evening progressed, and the literal tide of people poured into the centres, we were struck by how calm and composed the great majority of people were. There was no panic or no great demonstrations of angst; they simply wanted to know what they needed to do. Despite the constant pace and the sheer number of people, the evening progressed smoothly thanks to the many volunteers.

Again, the evacuations on Friday caught many people by surprise. The sheer number of people forced to leave their homes seemed both intimidating and impossible. Yet the volunteers still continued to man their posts even though many were evacuated themselves and had to leave to make their own arrangements. By this time, well experienced volunteers were able to meet people, greet them in a positive and knowing manner and direct them to where they needed to be. One lady who had been evacuated made the comment: "I am so glad you people are here. We had to leave our home in such a hurry. To arrive here and not know what to do would have just been too much."

Again, the unanimous consensus of all who volunteered at the doors of the Reception Centres was that people really took these events in stride. Only on Thursday, September 4, when the Joe Rich and Gallagher's Canyon areas had to be evacuated for a second time, did we notice that people had a kind of "war weariness" in that they had to go through all this again. Even then, good grace and gratitude prevailed.

One of the unique advantages of The Salvation Army is that it's an international organization with work in over 160 countries. In addition to an international set of resources, we also have both a national and provincial base of support to draw from. During our fire, a number of people from northern British Columbia came to help us out. One of our regular volunteers at the door, Mrs. Evelyn Burkatsky, was busily greeting and helping folks – just as she had in Kamloops and Vernon – working alongside a volunteer from northern B.C. He was astonished by how many people she seemed to know. Finally he asked, "Evelyn, do you know all these people?" Her reply was, "Oh no, but at a time like this you need to do your best and make everyone feel special."

During the Friday evacuations, an older man came towards Evelyn, obviously very upset. She approached him and asked what the matter was. He related how he'd come to Canada from the old country with nothing and had now lost everything. Evelyn realized that with many people coming in for assistance, this was not the ideal place to have the age old discussion of why bad things happen to good people, so she hugged the man and assured him that God was in control and somehow, he and his family would be all right. Evelyn shared that she had a Hungarian background and that her father had come from Budapest. On hearing this news, the man became ecstatic because he had come to Canada from Hungary. Well, there were hugs and kisses all around, and as he continued into the reception centre he said, "Now I know everything will be all right. The good Lord has sent me a Hungarian angel."

During the Thursday night evacuation, a volunteer who was a retired teacher from Rutland area schools noticed how the impact of the fire was bringing the community together. A young man came to the K.S.S. reception centre, and our worker recognized him as a former student. When asked if he could help, the young man replied that he had come to offer their home to anyone who was evacuated and needed accommodation. The rivalry between Rutland Secondary School and Okanagan Mission Secondary School has been intense and not always friendly, but old rivalries no longer mattered, what mattered were that neighbours were in need and people all over the city responded.

This caring was demonstrated by so many people in all the fires that hit our region. At a Reception Centre in Vernon, we witnessed a family come in during a late Sunday afternoon. A young girl came up to one of our volunteers and handed her some little pillows. She said these pillows were for children who had been evacuated. Her mom had helped her make them that afternoon. The touching part of this story was that this little girl had undergone a heart transplant just after Christmas. She had learned the importance of receiving care from others and now wanted to pass that on.

Thanks to the following volunteers for the background to this article: Les and Cathy Burrows, David Burrows, Nathan Burrows, Wayne and Sandra Gardner, Peter and Evelyn Burkatsky, Lorne and Donnie Graham, Caroline Goodman, Muriel Townsend, and many others who donated their time.

Reflections from the Trinity Hotel

by Delora Kuyvenhoven

When lightning struck a remote spot in Okanagan Mountain Park, Trinity Baptist Church was thrust into a rather unique role. Because of our size and central location, and because our senior pastor, Tim Schroeder, is chaplain to the Kelowna Fire Department, we were turned into a "hotel" and evacuee gathering centre. We housed and fed evacuees and firefighters for more than ten days, hosted debriefing sessions for those who lost their homes and became a hive of volunteer activity and coordination.

We thought we were ministering to others, but the truth is, the community ministered to us as well. We had so many offers of help. Businesses donated mattresses, sleeping bags, pillows and bedding. Local dentists gave us toothbrushes and toothpaste. People from the church and community continually dropped off toiletries and supplies as well as donations of money to help with the cost of housing and feeding the evacuees. And our volunteers were awesome. Working around the clock, they took on the role of running the "Trinity Hotel" extremely seriously. The terminology changed almost immediately: evacuees became guests; flowers were put in the rooms; chocolates were placed on the pillows every night and newspapers were left outside people's doors in the morning. And our guests very quickly became family.

The best part is that the Christian community rallied together to help. Many times we'd find volunteers, including pastors from other churches, wearing Trinity nametags and helping in our kitchen or making beds.

Eleven families from Trinity lost their homes. Some lost their home-based businesses as well. The Board of Deacons is now in the process of seeing how we, as a church, can help with the recovery process.

For those of us here in the Okanagan, August 2003 will go down in history as the summer of the big fire. Miraculously, no lives were lost and despite the physical devastation around us, our community is stronger and closer knit. We are working together to rebuild what was lost and we're finding people are open to spiritual things. At Trinity, we're excited about what God will do in the months ahead.

Let It Rain
by Gay Mentes

The fire raged on and on, one day coming closer to Kelowna, the next towards Penticton. The seriousness was mounting as the days went by. The thought crossed my mind I should volunteer to help. I had done some training a few years before in Winfield with Emergency Social Services, but when we relocated to Kelowna, I never did start going to their meetings here. However I still wanted to help if I could. Having never been in any major community emergency situation, I couldn't really visualize what this training was all about at the time, but now it was a reality. "Let it rain."

I was on the first shift of registering evacuees. These people had looks of shock, disbelief, and fear. Many had tears in their eyes as they told some of the most amazing stories. Folks arrived with chickens, boats, dogs, birds, cats and everything else imaginable. As fast as they arrived, day after day, churches and families and businesses began arriving and calling to volunteer housing, food, mats, water, pet care, clothes, sleeping bags, and much more. It was overwhelming to see the help pouring in. So many kind hearts, such concern, so many willing hands, it makes me wonder how beautiful heaven will be. "Let it rain."

Evacuees were in shock, some cheerful, others tearful. I don't recall seeing any anger in the few weeks of being at both registration centres. People were praying, swaying, staying; people chatted to strangers at the gas pumps, neighbours met for the first time. "Let it rain."

For days before my evacuation I carried around my photos and papers, each time going to do another shift at the Parkinson Rec. Centre, knowing the fire could be at my house before I got home. "Let it rain."

Sure enough, a few days later the alert came to our street and then evacuation! As evening approached on Friday, August 22, 2003, the sun set, folks were praying. Vehicles on our street were loading up in a scurry, we met neighbours we never met before. "Let it rain."

So, what is important? Our family, the dog, photos, important papers, and a few other things. The guys took computers and I went through my hope chest and took a few items, some clothes and a bit of food, a few odds and ends, my son's bike, etc. All we had to move things into was my little Firefly car and my husband's car. "Let it rain."

Out we would go with another load, then pause to look as the orange licking flames looked as if they would be here way too soon! Urgency set in. We were packing and praying and listening to the TV and radio and Castanet for moment to moment news. We stood out on the street and it started to sprinkle. There was lightning and thunder as if God spoke, saying "I am the only one who can put this fire out!!!" "Let it rain."

We went in to pack more and we heard that TV cameras which had for days been pointing towards the fire, were now just showing darkness, as if the fire had disappeared. I thought, no way! So I marched outside but to my surprise and disbelief, the flames were gone: no candling, no nothing! We shut the car doors then went in the house to watch the latest reports and we were no longer on the evacuation list. We went to bed and slept the whole night peacefully. "Let it rain."

Saturday August 20, 2003, I sat listening to Michael W. Smith's CD when the song 'Let it Rain' came on, which is based on Psalm 97. The words were just unbelievable! "Open the floodgates of Heaven, let it rain." I played it over and over... and one day soon, I will tell Michael W. Smith about the song's impact on my life that day. "Let it rain."

Many prayers were answered from all over the world. Amazing! It rained!

A few months later, the Kelowna Art Gallery asked for submissions of art pieces that showed reflections of the Okanagan Mountain Park Fire. Both my husband who is an artist and I – his shadow artist – submitted a piece. The opening was a healing moment in time for most of us, giving some closure.

The fire was an experience I never want to live through anytime soon, but thankfully, it rained!

Chapter Four
Watching and
Waiting

*"I am not an evacuee. I am not a volunteer.
I am a witness - a witness to the devastating
havoc wreaked by the forces of wildfire and
a witness to "man's humanity to man"…
if anything can unite us and forge common
bonds, it is the experience of the fire of 2003."*

NAN PELLATT

"I was left without words first in describing how far and fast the flames had travelled. I couldn't describe the hugeness of the flames. I was so close to this overpowering, overarching powerful image and yet I was as safe as kittens cuddled with their mother because the width of Okanagan Lake was between me and the fire."

RON SPENCE

ON THE STORM'S EDGE
BY BARBARA J. SHAVE

A hell fire is feeding on my city and its residents flee those ravenous jaws.

Although my neighbourhood remains eerily quiet, an orangey haze fills its narrow valley. I can make out only the outlines of the bordering hills and the sun is a blood-red Martian disk. It is as if my region is socked-in with winter ice-smog through which lazy snowflakes descend.

But in August, it snows ashes instead – flecks and slivers in black and white, and larger charred pieces of bark flutter down like dying dragonflies. Everything is quickly coated with this strange precipitation.

The thickened atmosphere muffles sound and the stillness accentuates the sense of foreboding. Even the birds have gone to roost in mid-day. This blanket of smoke bites the eyes and nose and cools the air like a storm cloud. It also brings on darkness before the bloody sun even sets. The scene is surreal and other-worldly and reminds me of an old movie about a nuclear winter.

It surely feels like the end of the world.

The June Springs Journals

by Amy Scovil-Lashinski

Editor's Note: email became an important method of keeping in touch with friends during the fire. The following are excerpts from Amy's emails.

FIRE UPDATE NUMBER 1- SUNDAY 24/08/03

Come rain, snow or fire, you can't keep me offline! I know you would all want to know the situation. Firstly we are all safe. We evacuated the horses and the dogs and ourselves last night. When Crawford Estates was evacuated we decided to move the two pregnant mares to our vet's in Winfield. Kevin left and I chose to stay behind and pack a few things.

All we could hear around us was sirens. Kevin arrived home and we loaded the two remaining horses, then he drove off to the vet's to dump them. By 11:30 p.m. I left our mountain.

The area we live in is mostly small farms with large animals, and Kelowna came out in droves to help BUT, I might also point out, the amount of lookey-loo's who came to watch our lives burning up was ridiculous. To be looking at areas you know you've driven or ridden on horseback in huge massive flames is such a surreal experience. It was the worst horror I had ever witnessed.

I headed straight for the emergency evacuation centre at K.S.S. where the people helping were wonderful. I registered Kevin, Cole and myself then headed over to my Nan's place and waited to hear back from Kevin, who had gone back to see if he could to grab a few more things. He phoned me at 1:15 a.m. and arrived at Nan's exhausted and in shock (despite what his manly image wants me to say) at 2 a.m. We have had so many offers of kindness and support that right now I think we are just overwhelmed.

FIRE UPDATE NUMBER 2 - MONDAY 25/08/03

Let me just first say that we are all still safe and so are the animals. The support from the volunteers, friends, family, firefighters and the community has been so incredible, it's probably the most emotional thing I face each day. If I ever doubted living in this town before, I never will now.

Friday at 5:45 p.m. Kevin got a call that our trainer in Joe Rich was on evacuation alert and she has well over a dozen horses at her place - plus a small herd of Jack Russells and a border collie. So off we went to haul horses.

Yesterday, Kevin was able to sneak back up to our house with the help of a 'secret angel.' Our house was fine, the 'secret angel' and his friends had turned the sprinklers on Saturday on our barn and surrounding area. Currently we don't know how our home fared or our neighbours. I pray the incredible firefighters and crew were able to hold this monster off, but at this point we can't see anything.

FIRE UPDATE NUMBER 3 - TUESDAY 26/08/08 DAY 5 OF EVACUATION

They were letting farmers with properties north of the power lines go check on their crops and such, so we quickly sent Kevin off... I mean last time I checked we were actively growing thistles... but we are apparently south of the power lines... at least we tried.

The regional district/forestry said crews were concentrating on our subdivision, the fire was at its strongest there and they were establishing fire lines. At 10:25 p.m., a typed thing at the bottom of the TV screen said you could currently see flames but it was no need for concern... yeah right! Concerned, I hopped out of bed and decided to drive around to see how close to our property the flames were. As I drove down K.L.O. Road, I could see the three bright lights from Gord's house still on, glowing away, so I could easily pin point where our home was. The bridge was no longer restricted, so I drove a bit further, feeling like a convict sneaking onto the prison grounds looking for the most ideal spot to scale the fence. At the big tree there was a road block. I asked how much further I could go. He said only to the East Kelowna Fire Hall.

Good or bad, the anticipation of wondering each and every day, is this the day we lose our house, is too much. The farmer's almanac is saying we won't get substantial rain until November... this is not what I really want to hear. Keep squishing those spiders!

P.S.: I still have NOT changed the date of the party as of yet... will keep you advised...

FIRE UPDATE NUMBER 4 - WEDNESDAY 27/08/03, DAY 6 OF EVACUEE-ISM

Yesterday our home was supposed to get gelled, but we aren't sure they got our place as they were supposed to be only gelling homes and not barns, sheds, or other structures that look like our house does... and when I hear the word gelled, am I only one that imagines the Ghost Busters movie where people were being slimed?

By the way, please let others know if they see a blonde who looks slightly distressed driving around in a black Barbie jeep with a pair of binoculars looking south east, that I am NOT a fire spectator, I'm just trying to keep track of my house.

At this point we are just trying to take guesses at when we will be allowed back home but the party is still on. I don't care at this point if we all meet at the road blockade, the party will go on!!!

I hope you've all got your yellow ribbons flying high. I have mine attached to my antenna - although at the rate I drive it has wrapped around it a few times and looks more like a yellow piece of garbage accidentally stuck to my antenna. I'm going to have to get something a bit different – maybe a bit of yellow toilet paper dragging from my heel will do the same thing! Will let you all know what's going on if we hear anything different today. Otherwise you know the drill, find your local rainmaker and beg him to flash-dance his soul out.

HOPEFULLY LAST UPDATE - THURSDAY 28/08/03

I just knew if I promised the local heroes that I wouldn't bake for them or subject them to my cooking that they would have our area mopped up in time for my party. I will be doing one last check on our home via the binoculars tonight, but as of yesterday, customers of ours at Dilworth were saying they could still see Gord's lights glowing and our roof on the barn standing.

We are days from heading home, a home that I probably won't bitch as much about now. God/goddess/whatever it is you believe in, bless us all and thank you.

SUNDAY, AUGUST 31ST AND STILL NOT IN

Everyone else is back into their homes or neighbourhoods except for approximately 70 people in June Springs Road area. At this point, I think they found Ron and Edna's homemade wine stash, and are enjoying it while they relax their muscles in the hot tubs on all the properties up there.

I went up when they opened the road Saturday for residents from 10 am to 4 p.m. The barn and shop were just fine. They hadn't been gelled and there appeared to be no damage from anyone or any flying debris. But let me tell you, (wink, wink) I was shocked to find my three story log home levelled down to just the basement... (cough, cough, insurance, cough). They hadn't gelled the bunker/house either.

As I was changing my hubs to drive up the front, a water truck had just come down. He said although the fire was a bit away, it was still way too close for us to let down our guard. And as we have been hearing all along, it all depends on the winds.

TUESDAY 02/09/03 DAY 13 - YES THIRTEEN AS IN ALMOST A HALF A MONTH...

We are still out, and (deep sigh) the party will have to be postponed. At this point even if they let us home, I have my suspicions that they won't let anyone other than residents up there. The back road is now a freeway of heavy machinery. A large semi truck with a tanker of fire retardant foam or whatever was on its way up, only to slow to a stop on a hill and have all its weight shift to the back of the tanker and make it so he couldn't go anywhere. So, I took this opportunity to take some of the drivers a pop and get some information direct from the front line workers. I was told that the fire was three kilometres up the hill and two to three kilometres over... way way too close for comfort. He said the fire had gotten so big again that it was creating its own wind and it was travelling down to our place. He also had said the water bombers I had seen weren't actually scheduled to be there. They'd had to evacuate the ground crew and bring in the air fighters... that if I saw bombers up there it really wasn't a good sign.

Around 4 p.m. we saw the Martin Mars bomber in all its glory flying JUST over us. They were so low, I'm sure I could make out the pilot mouthing "GET THE HELL OUTTA THERE LADY !!!"

WEDNESDAY 03/09/03 DAY 14 - 2 WEEKS - 336 HOURS- 20160 MINUTES

I called the fire information line today and was told I should probably start looking for long term housing... ah hello, when did we go from day passes to spending the winter out of our homes? I think we are coming to the 'it's not so much fun anymore' part of this event, Kevin and I are arguing over milk (just laugh with me and say, oh Amy you're right again), the dogs aren't eating, and at school today under the heading "What I Hope To Do This Year," Cole wrote, see my house.

Well I think that's it for this update, not too perky huh... but let's see you all be Miss Sweet and Charming after living like a nomad for 2 weeks... the survivor people have NOTHING on me!!!! Okay so I don't have to eat bugs or barbequed rats, but at least after the tribal boot off ceremony they get to go back to the same old beach.

THURSDAY 04/09/03 DAY 15

Another day... another gray hair... I believe it was yesterday I was complaining bitterly about not being allowed back – well I guess they DO know what they are doing on the fire lines!!! Another large area of East Kelowna into Joe Rich was evacuated again last night.

This morning we are assuming by all accounts our home is still standing. Out of the 18 Kettle Valley Trestles they lost two last night and the chances sound slim to save the others. Sorry not too cheery this time, just a bit unnerving all over again. Here's hoping winds throw it back on itself.

FRIDAY 05/09/03 - DAY 16

Sorry you all, it hasn't been a good day for us today. Forestry contacted us and asked if they could build a fire guard around the house and barn. The fire is close and they are expecting category six firestorm behaviour later today and tomorrow. They are trying their best to keep the fire away from our buildings, but the gel isn't sticking to the logs, and this fire guard is about our last resource.

Sorry for the shortness and lack of humour but just not so sure what's going on and in a bit of shock here, I mean this started near Rattlesnake Island... who would have predicted it would be at our home?

MONDAY 08/09/03 WE CAN GO HOME !!!!

We can go home we can go home we can go home !!! Wheeeee HAAAAAA !!!! We still are on alert and Thursday they are calling for winds, but for now we can at least spend a night at home!

TUESDAY 09/09/03 DAY 19

We are back at home finally. The evacuation order has been lifted and changed to an alert and other than being inundated with stink bugs (nasty disgusting creatures - sure like to see those on Fear Factor going down someone's throat), we have gotten through this pretty unscathed.

The back of the property is now a freeway for logging and skidding vehicles. They have stripped our trees up to the second turn going towards the trestles, then down along the back of our property. Kevin thinks it's quite a scar... but I think we now have a hell of a path set up for some good sledding action. Maybe instead of a summer party we'll wait for winter and have a sledding party!

Take care,

Amy, Kevin and Cole

Life in a War Zone

by Meryl Duprey

On the night of August 22, I stood on the side road that runs along the eastern edge of Mt. Boucherie, an extinct volcano, and watched through field-glasses as more than 200 homes burned to the ground and 26,000 people fled from the eastern flank of the city. I could now distinguish the black pall of a burning house from the lighter smoke of the forest fire.

The inferno was hanging in sickening proximity above the Kettle Valley subdivision and it was impossible to distinguish spot fires from street-lights. I handed the field-glasses to my nine-year-old son, who peered with confusion. I'm not sure if he understood and I didn't feel the urge to enlighten him.

The first day we hardly noticed the small trail of smoke to the southeast. Subsequently the fire became the number one tourist attraction in the Okanagan. Driving became doubly hazardous as onlookers watched the blaze instead of oncoming traffic and smoke dropped visibility to something like dense fog.

The fire would doze sometimes only to revive within a couple of hours. But the smoke was always omnipresent. It had begun as a pleasant spice in the breeze, eventually becoming a constant burning sensation in the backs of our throats. It obscured all views, permeated our houses and clothing and dropped the outside temperature by 15 degrees. The sun was replaced by a red ball that would fade in and out of view. On the night of August 21, the fire had reached the area directly across the lake from our home, glowing from within a pall of smoke that reached so high into the atmosphere that the top was capped with ice clouds like the anvil of a thunderhead. At noon, the streetlights were on. That evening eleven houses burned to the ground as firefighters were forced to flee a wall of flame 150 metres high. The Kelowna Fire Department issued a tearful apology. The public sense was that someone had failed. I remembered talking to an old man in Peachland. He explained how he had seen the lightning strike that had precipitated the fire. "They had the thing out," he said, "and then they just took off and left it to smoulder. They knew better."

A hippyfriend of mine blamed global warming.

Watching the houses burn, I remembered a walk through the streets of Kettle Valley. The yards, as I recalled, were like paintings from a suburban fable, replete with built-in sprinklers and lawns so recently sown you could still see the outlines of the sod-squares. In the driveways there were SUVs tugging trailers loaded with motorcycles and jet-skis. They were the quintessential symbols of everything Kelowna stands for – fun, carefree and profitable. That day, I had looked at them with outsider disdain. My little trailer in Westbank was the kind of thing these people had probably fought to escape. Watching those houses burn transformed my disdain into despair.

I had felt similarly watching the World Trade Towers fall in New York City during the 9/11 terrorist attack. Sure, they were symbolic of everything I hated – the centre of a mega-mall that was turning half the world into Wal-mart customers and the other half into refugees. But as long as those towers were standing even those of us who lived on society's fringes could wake up in the morning with the confidence that we would not be running for our lives in the wake of some uncontrolled destruction.

On the morning of August 22, many homes had burned to the ground, yes, but not nearly as many as had been originally reported. The fire seemed to be under control. The "night of hell" was over and we could all count ourselves lucky that nothing worse had occurred.

As the afternoon approached I heard the wind-chimes on our porch and was surprised to see the other side of Okanagan Lake for the first time in days. The wind was bending the treetops as I jumped into the car and drove down the street to my mother's house. "Can I borrow your police scanner?" I asked. "I think something is going to happen." Early weather reports had suggested wind was coming and such an occurrence might make the fire more volatile. The scanner would tell me more than the local media outlets. I heard the voice of Kelowna Fire Department captain Len Moody. He sounded controlled and focused. He was talking to a group of men who were trapped in Bertram Creek Park. They were surrounded by flames.

"We're making a stand on Curlew Drive!" a frantic voice kept shouting. Those on Curlew Drive would eventually be cut off as well. They would struggle to keep their supply of water from being shut down, a worst-case scenario that seemed more and more likely as the fire progressed that afternoon. Although no one was talking about the consequences at the time, it would later qualify as a miracle that those on Curlew had not lost their lives.

I turned on the television and noticed the talking heads still comforting the public with assertions that no houses were on fire. Perhaps they really didn't know, I decided, or maybe they were trying to reserve their knowledge, hoping that these reports, like the one that had verified 25 homes lost the night before, were greatly exaggerated. The scanner came alive with firemen calling frantically for support at the junction of Crawford Road and Stewart Road. I looked on my Kelowna map and realized with growing dread that the fire had pushed well inside the boundaries of the city. When a radio voice reported flames spotted at the junction of Raymer and Gordon Drive – only a minute from the downtown core – my mother got up from her chair and started crying.

The day after the fire consumed hundreds of homes, my wife and I were driving back from Kelowna. Little groups of soldiers could be seen wandering along the highway that runs through the city. The downtown was eerily quiet for an August Sunday. Then the radio announcer directed our attention to the area just north of Westbank. A new fire had broken out. We hurried home and watched as black smoke started to fill the sky above our house. My mother called, instructing us to start packing our essential belongings.

That was when I realized we would never be able to observe smoke on the horizon again with the faith that it would not blossom into a raging inferno and eventually turn us into refugees. This has nothing to do with the ability or lack thereof ascribed to the firefighting services in our area.

The debate that's already beginning about this issue in Kelowna is the normal reaction of human beings trying to find a justification for their failure to protect themselves.

Water bombers would eventually attack the small Westbank fire with unprecedented ferocity. It would be out within an hour thanks to having most of British Columbia's firefighting capability stationed in our area.

Such is life in the war zone.

A friend from Williams Lake called, hysterical after seeing the headline, "Westbank in Flames" on one of the news networks. Her sister called from New Brunswick, having heard that 10,000 people were evacuated from Kelowna. "That's 26,000," my wife corrected reluctantly.

Nothing will address our terror. We all learned in Kelowna on the night of August 22 that we are not in control, no matter how much money we spend or how high we build our walls.

At the time of writing, the Okanagan Mountain Fire is sleeping fitfully. My mother still has her belongings packed in her car, due to the daily reports of spot-fires within several kilometres of where we live. The weather report is for hot and dry.

Today is a Gift
by John Guidolin

I vividly remember Aline and I looking at the kilometre-long fire across the lake and saying it was "neat," something we would never again see. Six days later we would lose our house, more than 15 kilometres away from those flames.

On Tuesday, August 19, various areas in Kelowna were on evacuation alert, but the fire was a considerable distance away. We began what became a bit of a ritual… staring at the fire until all hours of the night and day… watching the fire come closer – three mountain ranges away then two mountain ranges away – still in awe and not really thinking it was going to be a threat.

On Thursday evening Aline, Gabrielle and I were at a school basketball meeting when the coach received a call to "let the Crawford families know their area is on alert." We arrived home by about 8:30 p.m. and the fire was at the top of the closest mountain range. Water bombers and helicopters were going steady all day. We had a few things packed. Typical of children, Benjamin packed his Playstation, toothbrush and a special picture album and Gabrielle packed sports bags of clothes while wearing her winter jacket and boots. We sent them back … Gabrielle to put stuff back and Ben to pack clothes. At 10:30 p.m. we received the evacuation order. A weird and eerie silence descended on the entire neighbourhood. Everyone was packing vehicles. We packed a few more things and headed to the Casorso Ranch… friends we met two years ago when we moved to Kelowna.

We stayed up most of the evening helping the Casorsos pack as they were now on one-hour alert. We stared at the fire while watching a steady stream of vehicles come by from our subdivision. We woke up to what seemed a calmer Friday morning.

We registered at Parkinson Recreation Centre and an advisory was issued that we would be allowed back into our homes from 10 a.m. to 1 p.m. By the time we got the permit we had about an hour, but we had about everything out we wanted and still did not think anything was going to happen.

We put the garbage out.

Gabrielle and Ben were awesome in getting pictures off the walls. Aline had done an excellent job of organizing our crawl space with Rubbermaid bins everywhere. Gabrielle tried to sneak out a few more clothes but hey, "We are coming back soon!" As we left our house for what would be the last time I remember that weird and eerie silence once again. Like a ghost town.

Friday afternoon... back to the Casorsos'. Everything calm. Around 5 p.m. the winds picked up considerably. Large pieces of debris were landing in the Casorsos' yard. Then chaos set in when we were told to evacuate from the Casorso house in 10 minutes.

We retreated to the Coast Capri Hotel. By now the south mountain ranges and skies were ablaze and close to 30,000 people were evacuated! Firestorm Friday was upon us. To quote a magazine article: "Gusting winds have suddenly whipped the Okanagan Mountain Park Fire into a frenzy. Flames leap hundreds of feet into the night sky advancing on Kelowna like a legion of demons released from hell."

We stood on the balcony and watched... and watched... and watched. While we could not see our subdivision directly we could see the fire and smoke hundreds and hundreds of feet into the night sky... every once in a while the smoke turning darker... meaning another house gone.

Many people asked how we were and the word numb is the term I used. Saturday morning we woke to newspaper headlines, "Houses Burning; Hundreds Possibly Destroyed."

A few families met at Aline's brother's home where someone saw a breaking story on CHBC from a cameraman who entered the Crawford area and videotaped the destroyed houses. He spoke of the incredible sights he saw. The room quieted as we tried to get a glimpse of our house. The cameraman said he was in the area for three hours so we continued to watch segments, hoping to catch a glimpse of our houses.

I thought to myself, the cameraman must have more video tape. Danny Ruggiero, Tim Lenardon and I went to the studios to see if we could see more video. I thought there would be a lineup at the front entrance. We agreed to be interviewed while they were sorting through and showing us the tapes. The cameraman confirmed all homes destroyed were above the power lines, so we were pretty sure Timmy's house was OK, although there were still rumours of flying embers hitting houses throughout the neighbourhood. Dan's house was just below the power lines and our house was just above so the adrenaline began to flow.

The cameraman began by showing where he entered the subdivision and it looked like a normal everyday drive until you hit the park and the power lines! He had the camera pointing across the street from our house and the first house we saw was destroyed. I tried to explain the location of our house relative to the park and although he did not come out and say it, just by his reaction, I had the feeling our house was gone.

He continued to fast forward and located the Ruggiero house. From a distance it looked like Dan and Debbie's house was OK. He then located a tape to try and identify our house. The video was getting closer but the tape stopped just before our lot. I studied the last frame of tape for an eternity. I could see our neighbour's house across the street but from the angle of the shot should I be able to see it? Should my house be blocking the view? How far back was my house?

The City organized a meeting for residents of the affected areas. When Fire Chief Zimmermann walked into the room he was given a standing ovation. It is a moment etched in my memory which still gives me chills and brings tears to my eyes. Maps and addresses were handed out confirming the 238 houses destroyed on Firestorm Friday.

Although somewhat prepared, to actually see 1503 Woodridge on the handout was a bit overwhelming. Inviting all neighbours who lost their homes and those who did not was truly comforting for us.

Tuesday evening the city provided three double-decker buses to the Crawford area for families who lost their homes. I can best describe the atmosphere as nervous humorous. Our house was first and everyone noticed the garbage had not been picked up. That seemed to break the ice for everyone on the bus. We were not allowed to get off the bus and with our house being elevated we could not see too much other than the mass destruction.

As the tour continued, families took turns telling the bus driver to stop. Everyone gave families space to view their house, a bit of quiet time and a few tears. Then usually they noted something amazing or something that survived. House after house, the mass destruction was amazing. As we were coming to the last few houses we came across six firemen at work putting spot fires out. The bus slowed down and simultaneously everyone began clapping and cheering. The firefighters all looked, acknowledged our admiration saying sorry, a few with tears running down their cheeks.

On the 27th the city allowed residents of evacuated areas to go back home but everyone still remained on evacuation alert. This was our first opportunity to walk up our driveway and view the devastation up close. It was truly amazing the destruction from the heat and the fire...charred remains of Gabrielle's bed, Ben's scooter, bicycles, lawn mower, exercise bike, appliances, dishes... but mostly rubble and ash.

We visited and stared at the rubble for eight weeks waiting for it to be taken away. When it finally happened reality set in a bit.

Those sixty days taught us many things. We learned that everyone reacts differently. We learned how lucky we are to have a very supportive family, awesome friends, great colleagues, clients, and community. The outpouring of support has been tremendous.

I heard a quote recently that had special meaning. Maybe something we can all live by.

"Slow down a bit and enjoy what is around us...
Today is a gift. That is why it is called the *present*."

The Irony of Looking for Boxes

by Chris Kasianchuk

I was driving back from the dump Saturday morning. My car had been crammed with flattened cardboard boxes, limp bubble wrap and crumpled newspapers which had, for the previous month, held and protected every single thing we owned. Some of those boxes hadn't been unpacked in 20 years – they'd remained sealed for their entire tour of Toronto storage lockers, crawl spaces and apartment closets. Now that we'd moved back west and found our dream home in Naramata, it was time to unpack everything.

Once I had emptied everything into the appropriate containers, I slowly drove down the switchback road that led from the landfill, trying to determine exactly which combination of elation, melancholy and terror best described the way I felt leaving those last vestiges of our Toronto life in metal bins beside a dump in Penticton.

That's when I saw the fire.

You don't see forest fires in downtown Toronto. Car fires, maybe. But as soon as I saw that solid white plume rising from the dark forest of Okanagan Mountain Park I knew exactly what it was. Forest fires had been burning all around us since we'd moved. In Keremeos, in Barriere and in Washington state. And their smoke had filled the valley. It was only a matter of time until the Okanagan got its own. I pulled to the side of the road to watch the water bombers, but there were none. Only that little finger of dense, white smoke.

I proceeded home along the twists of Naramata Road. At every rise and clearing, my eyes searched for the plume. For a moment I even thought that perhaps I was the first one to see the fire – maybe it had just started and I should call 911. There was nothing on the radio about it – maybe no one had noticed.

Of course, everyone had noticed. When I whipped down to the general store, it's all they were talking about. "Started by lightning about 3 a.m.," someone said. "The Mars is on its way," said another, referring to that flying beast that can dump the equivalent of a small town's yearly water supply on a single hotspot. But the Mars didn't come that day, nor did anyone else. The finger of smoke I'd seen from the dump had grown to an entire hand by the end of the day and as evening fell, it was lit from below by orange flames.

At dawn the next day, I walked to the corner of our property with my four-year-old son to survey the fire's progress. It was astounding. It was easily 10 times the size of the day before. Smoke now billowed from half the mountainside. The fire had grown large enough that updates were available on the radio. We watched the water bombers complete cycle after cycle, from lake to fire, with little effect. Their payloads seemed to evaporate in midair.

By Monday it was obvious that the Okanagan Mountain Park Fire was not only out of control but a major concern for Naramata. As the blaze trundled its way toward Chute Lake, less than 20 kilometres away, my wife and I took a crash course in fire preparedness. We cleaned the gutters, cut down trees that were too close to the house and stocked up on batteries, water, and candles. Ironically, I had to go into Penticton for boxes for our valuables, which we then stowed in our car, ready to go at a moment's notice.

The process of paring our possessions down to what we could fit in our car was made simple by the fact we'd just moved. Everything was already sorted and organized. It wasn't until I went across the street to check our elderly neighbours that I realized what a unique position we were in. To us, our house was still just a building with our stuff in it. Stuff that insurance could replace should the worst come to pass. Having moved in less than a month before, we'd had no time to invest any emotional capital. To our neighbours, their house was home. Four walls and a roof containing decades of memories; generations of lives and loves. There's no insurance for that.

I helped them clear some brush and let them know that we were there to help if they needed it. They smiled and thanked me, but there was a resignation in their response – a knowledge that any effort they put in would fall far short of saving what needed to be saved.

As the fire grew so did the media coverage. Every one of our friends in Toronto now knew exactly where we lived. The only thing that kept our phone from ringing off the hook was the fact that the line went dead from time to time. Then the power became unreliable – off and on several times a day. Water use was strictly curtailed. The fire was choking us off.

When we woke Tuesday morning it looked as if it had snowed overnight. It wasn't snow, of course – it was ash. There were burnt needles falling from the sky. When I walked to the corner of our property I couldn't see 50 feet through the smoke. We had difficulty breathing. Fire trucks and heavy equipment from all over B.C. emerged from the haze as if by magic. Presto! A pumper truck from Saanich. Abracadabra! A bulldozer from Richmond. They sped past and then disappeared into the smoke, on their way to the Naramata Fire Hall and beyond to Chute Lake Road where they were making their stand.

Wednesday morning at 3 a.m., a volunteer on the Fire Preparedness Committee rang our doorbell to give us our one-hour evacuation alert. Even though we were packed and ready to go it sent a chill through me. To think that a force of nature more powerful than anything I'd ever seen was within striking distance of destroying nearly everything I owned was terrifying. I did not go back to bed. Instead I stood outside in the dark and watched the pulsating glow of the oncoming fire.

There is a horrible majesty to an inferno that size. It creates its own atmosphere, its own winds. Every afternoon, almost like clockwork, the fire's convection would suck its own smoke up into the stratosphere creating a pillar of smoke and ash five miles high. It billowed and churned over on itself like Hawaiian surf and even in the blinding sunshine, glowed orange from the flames below.

Thursday brought winds of change and there's never been a truer phrase. The fire did an abrupt about-face and burned towards Kelowna where it ultimately ravaged over 200 homes.

The valley was still full of smoke, but that eerie glow on the horizon, like 10,000 torches held by strangers, was gone. For the next few days our car remained packed and ready to go but in our bones we knew the danger had passed.

A SMOKE SCREENED MEMORY RETOLD MUCH LATER BY ERIN MILLAR

(an excerpt from *Photographs of Orange Summer*)

My mother was
ideal aged wine, 27 years, knee
deep in Okanagan Lake, one piece
bathing suited, bought at the five-and-dime. An orange
sun was seated

on her head.
My father said
he would never
forget how beautiful she was.

The truth is
sunlight is
always copper in August.

Smoke
canopies the valley from fires burning dry sage.

Smoke
is a tangerine filter on an 1980s manual camera.

Smoke
was a pair of cheap orange colored shades
on my father's nose, through which he
saw my onepiecebathingsuited mother.

Smoke
that painted the most stunning
sunset I have ever captured was from
fire that burnt
300 homes last summer.

Watching and Waiting
by Amber Marsh

On Saturday, August 16, my mother and father in-law and I were down at Bertram beach. It had started to cloud over and the wind was really blowing, but we were determined to get out in the water, so we inflated our floating chairs and cast off into the lake. The wind was making such big waves, we had to hold onto each other with the last person holding a buoy so we wouldn't drift back into shore. We noticed a big puff of smoke coming from just around the bend. We wrote it off to fires in Washington, but there was that nagging worry in the back of my mind, that smoke looked awfully close.

My boss is the Volunteer Fire Chief here in Kelowna. He and his men were called out to help battle the fire on Monday. On Tuesday afternoon, he poked his head into my office and said, "You live up near Kettle Valley, right?" I responded "Yes, why?" He answered, "You know you are on evacuation alert now."

I headed home immediately but I don't even really remember that drive; I think I stopped at the stop signs, and red lights... but I couldn't say so with conviction. When I got home I packed a bag of clothes – enough for three days – and loaded all our photo albums, negatives, important papers and yearbooks into our car. I felt a bit better after doing that.

We sat around listening to the radio trying to get as much information as possible. One lady called in saying if she lived where we did, she would grab her kids and pets and get the hell out of there. That kind of freaked me out.

That evening we walked up to Kettle Valley and watched the orange glow in the sky. We couldn't see any flames on the ridge we'd marked as the "time to get worried ridge," but it was still amazing to see the sky lit up like that.

I didn't go into work on Wednesday. We have two dogs and two birds, and I work by Reid's corner, a 25 minute drive. I didn't want to be a half hour away if the order came down. We just hung around the house listening to the radio, taking hourly walks up to Kettle Valley to see if we could see anything. We couldn't. After dinner we walked out again and trees were candling on the "time to get worried" ridge. We watched transfixed as gusts of wind would cause the glow to increase, then it would calm. There were a lot of people out doing the same thing we were. Watching and waiting.

Sean's brothers arrived later that night. They had made plans to visit us and decided that, fire or no fire, they were coming. All it really meant now, though, was that we had more people in our house to be evacuated should the need arise.

Thursday I went to work until lunchtime, spending most of the morning answering questions from concerned co-workers. I can't even count how many people offered me use of their spare rooms, garages, or yards to keep our dogs. I was overwhelmed by the compassion I received. After work, we were planning to have roast chicken, but it wasn't going to be ready for a while so I crashed. When I woke up, we walked up to Kettle Valley. What I saw blew me away. The fire had done exactly what we didn't want it to; it had moved along the ridge behind Kettle Valley, crested it and was moving directly towards us. As we turned to head home, an RCMP car pulled up beside us and ordered us back to our houses. I knew then, the evacuation order was coming.

We got everyone and everything into the car within half an hour. We drove down the road, a red glow in our rearview mirror. When we rounded the corner that led down the hill, I looked up the forestry road and saw trees candling at the summit. The fire had very quietly moved along behind our community and was coming down with our home directly in its path.

It's quite funny really, but what I remember most about that evening is Sean's mom grabbing the roasted chicken saying "I'm not leaving this full chicken behind." She threw it, a bowl of potatoes, the salad and some stuffing into grocery bags and took it with her. I never did eat dinner that night.

Sean and I went down to K.S.S. to register and ended up getting a room at the Sandman Inn. They let us keep our dogs in our room with us. Knowing they were okay was all that mattered to me. We watched the news until after midnight when we basically fell asleep exhausted. Around 6:30 a.m., we woke up and clicked the TV back on. We heard homes had been lost in the Rimrock area. We got a call from my boss saying he had taken a drive up around our place, and that everything was looking good up there.

The next evening, we stared transfixed at the TV watching subdivisions being engulfed in flame. The reporters couldn't even speak. In each shot, we tried to find landmarks to orient ourselves. We saw what we thought was the brick gym building in Kettle Valley... our eyes moved across the screen... and all there was where our house would be was flames and dark black smoke. "That's it," I thought, "our house is gone." I could hardly breathe. Sean and I held onto each other, 99% convinced our house was gone. How could it possibly still be there? Not wanting to eat, but knowing we had to, we went to a restaurant for dinner. A family in the booth across from us asked if we had been evacuated. They were from out of town and had been vacationing here for years. Sean had ordered a steak with Caesar salad. The waitress came to tell them there was no steak left for the father's steak and eggs. Sean said, "If mine was the last steak, you can give it to him for his steak and eggs, I'll just have chicken instead." It's one of those things so minor and so silly to remember, but all I thought was, here we are, at the lowest moment in our life to date, and Sean was still being so kind and giving up his steak for this stranger. We went back to the hotel and I cried off and on for hours, eventually crying myself to sleep, with Sean holding me saying "it's only things, it's only stuff."

Saturday morning we bought some binoculars, drove across the bridge to Westbank and tried to see through the smoke if we could see our house, or what was left of it. We couldn't, there were too many trees in our area, and all we could see was the devastation of Viewcrest and Okaview. Reluctantly, I called my boss to see if he had possibly been fighting the fire anywhere near our house and might know its status. I woke him up. He had just come off over 40 hours on the front lines, (he had been on Viewcrest that night). He didn't know how our house was and we were resigned to wait until the Sunday meeting at Trinity Baptist Church, where they would hand out maps and deal the blows.

And then the call came in late Saturday evening from my boss. All he said was, "Your house made it." The shock in his voice was audible. Our home was still there. Really by what can only be described as a miracle, our house had survived Firestorm Friday.

On Sunday we went to the church, wanting to be sure, needing to be sure my boss hadn't made a mistake. Once there, we saw neighbours who'd heard news they had lost their house directly across the street from us.

Monday, we woke up to discover our car had been broken into. Our jubilance was dashed by the act of some mindless, cowardly criminal preying on misfortunate times. This combined with the stress of the past few days broke us. We escaped to Edmonton, to our family and friends.

On September 1st, we drove up to our house for the first time in 10 days. Until we rounded the corner where the forestry road was, everything looked fine but then it hit me; the devastated trailer park and one house standing, then three lots with nothing but chimneys and burnt sticks, then a house and then our house, then four more lots of nothing. On our side of the street maybe five homes remained. Over 30 homes in our direct area had been destroyed.

When we got out of the car in our driveway, I had two incredibly strong emotions flowing through me: joy at our house escaping the fire virtually unscathed and then this even heavier emotion of unbearable guilt. Why us?

I still drive up the road blown away by what happened, feeling relief at not having to rebuild our lives and the guilt of escaping this tragedy when so many others did not. Our house still carries the lingering smell of smoke, and I still dream sometimes of that night we fled our neighbourhood. But in time, those will fade, the smell will fade, the neighbourhood will rebuild and we will know that we can face anything after surviving this.

Chapter Five
Finding Strength in Each Other

"Never, from a lifelong journalistic overview of my own participation in the coverage of various disasters, have I experienced a community crisis response so caring, total and united as that generated by this great city we call home. Our citizens were bonded as brothers and sisters."

WALLY DENNISON

E-MAIL OUT: *"To all religious, non-religious, formerly religious friends, please keep praying."*

E-MAIL IN: *"Add 'newly religious' and I am on it. Be brave tomorrow – our thoughts are with you constantly."*

DEB AND VALERIE

THE STRENGTH OF A TEENAGER

BY DEBORAH MATHESON

The increasing urgency of the telephone calls from our 19-year-old daughter, who was home alone, sent us packing up early from the Salmon Arm music festival. Ash was coming down during the open air event from the Chase fire.

After a first hand look at the Osoyoos fire a week before and the fact there were now hundreds of fires burning in B.C., I quickly slipped into panic mode while my new husband calmly drove back to Kelowna. The fire was making national news and they were mentioning streets and parks very close to our home. The drive felt like the longest two hours of my life.

Strangely enough, we could see no sign of the fire when we pulled into town or as we neared our subdivision in the southern end of the city where the fire was reportedly encroaching. Our daughter apologized for over-reacting. Though hugely relieved to see us, she decided to go back to her friends now that we were home. I felt a bit foolish.

The next day was one of several that was eerily calm and smoky and oppressively hot. The fire was masked, at least during the day and we tried to believe that everything would be okay. Heather carried on with her plans to go to Tofino that evening with friends. We got ready to return to work after our month-long honeymoon.

On Monday the smoke cleared and my panic returned. The massive fire was visible for the first time. A few people were being evacuated but there was still hope the wind would shift and the fire would soon burn back upon itself and go out. The few helicopters that were flying overhead with their buckets looked almost silly in their attempts to douse the massive, fast spreading flames.

The next day at work I began listening to the radio and for the next few weeks relied extensively on it and the web site. Heather was getting the news in Tofino and she was keeping in very close touch during a time when she would normally be completely removed from her family, having a great time with her friends before they headed in different directions in September.

Tuesday was a day of mixed emotions: relief that the wind was pushing the fire towards Naramata and empathy that the lovely little town might once again be facing a huge fire as it had in 1993. Then, with my guard down and spirits lifting a bit, I heard on the radio that we were placed on one hour evacuation notice.

Friends helped us pack music, photos, and pictures and we shipped them off to what we thought would be a safe haven (they were also evacuated later) but we still believed this was just a big inconvenience.

The thick smoke returned and we spent the next two days in our own haze as we listened to the unbelievable spread of the fire and the destruction of our park. How was it possible? Just a few weeks earlier we had been happily married in our yard overlooking our property with the massive ponderosa pines. Our friends and family had travelled from across the country and celebrated with us all week in our wonderful valley.

The evacuation notice sat beside the thank-you notes we were still writing and the pictures that were still arriving. The neighbours were busy watering down cedar shake roofs while we were silently thankful we had just replaced ours with fire resistant material.

We were beginning to relax on Thursday evening, about to enjoy a late dinner, when dozens of sirens blared and the telephone rang with an out-of-town friend who had just been at our house, telling us we had to get out. The phone continued to ring as we found our cat and grabbed the remaining important things we thought we needed.

Heather returned the next day, joined us at our second evacuee home along with another family of four and a number of cats. She couldn't believe what had happened in the few days she was gone and was distraught, angry, and confused about what to do.

That night, after several frantic trips to move our belongings and help others evacuate, the three of us went to the beach under the bridge and watched the homes burn down. I refused to believe that ours was one of them until later that evening when they reported the numbers and the street names. Only four lost in the new, flat, tree-less subdivision where we thought they might be able to bring it under control, but more than 100 on our beautiful tree-lined streets.

I gave up hope while Heather called our house and left a message telling it to be brave and strong and that we would return soon. Though optimistic and supportive beyond her years, I sunk into despair while we waited for that dreadful visit to the church to receive the news.

She sat between us at the church and extracted a promise from us. No matter what, her stepdad and I had to be okay, whatever the news. Yes, it was the house she grew up in, yes she had picked it out when she was five years old, yes all of her belongings were there gathered and ready to be moved to her first apartment, yes she loved the neighbourhood and the hills and the trees but all she really cared about was that we would be alright because we mattered so much more.

We agreed and held hands to seal the pact.

The list arrived. Our house had been brave and strong and a teenager's strength had pulled us through a terrible ordeal.

Who is the Hero?

by MCpl Don Miller

I volunteered to go to the Okanagan and do what I could to fight the forest fire, not because of the fact both my parents were born and raised there and most of my dearest relatives still call it home; it wasn't because every summer my family now visits the beautiful Okanagan Valley to vacation, camp, hike and water-ski; it wasn't because of my childhood fascination with the Ogopogo. Nor was it because of how awestruck in wonder I was when I first hiked along the Myra Canyon Trestles. I did it because I could. Duty.

To a soldier in the Canadian Forces, there are not always a lot of perks. We are not highly paid and we are rarely furnished with the best possible equipment to accomplish the mission, but we are well respected within our own community, nation, and world. We travel throughout the planet in an attempt to eradicate injustice and bring peace, hope, and prosperity to those without. We willingly place ourselves at the risk of injury or death in the most horrible, terrifying places on the planet. Why? Duty. When duty calls, we are there. Without question, without hesitation or second thoughts.

What made our efforts in Kelowna different than any job I've ever done before was the fact that people cared and were immensely grateful. I've never been someone's hero before. I've never been blown kisses or waved at by grateful crowds enroute to my work. Thank you.

People of Kelowna, for the honour you have shown me, thank you for your gratitude and your respect. For those two weeks the people of Kelowna seemed like a family to me. The world would be a better place if they could see how you all worked together and helped each other out in your time of despair.

If I had any words of wisdom to give you, it would be to remember, remember what this devastation meant to you and how you came together to combat it. How you reached out to one another. How you were strong. And remember how bad it hurt.

If you always remember these emotions, you can have cause to celebrate them. Because while the firefighters, soldiers, loggers and equipment operators are strong and brave, the real heroes are you: the men and women of Kelowna.

Scorched Forests: Fertile Soil for Community Rebirth

by Stephanie Sanders on behalf of the Sanders family

I was home. Not much had changed in my refuge. The living room sat as quietly as ever while the kitchen teamed with life. Yet, out of the corner of my eye, a strange box caught my attention. Why on earth would all the photos be packed up in a box in the family room? My father answered, telling us of a lightning strike down the lake. It only started that morning and so we laughed at my parents' cautious reaction to gather their precious belongings. But with each hour, the dark cloud that rose above the inferno instilled an ominous feeling in my mind.

A few days passed and the feeling of laughter turned to terror. Then, the terror was laced with panic. After this ended, true terror I had never experienced firsthand filled my dreams, waking me every night as I ran endlessly from the flames.

"They will stop it. The bombers will come. This is the Okanagan. The winds will die down."

But they did not.

It was unbearable to have nothing to do but breathe smoke-filled air and wait. I considered volunteering as the first wave of evacuations began, but immediately I knew that was not our role. We were doomed to be the ones standing in lines waiting for someone to explain it all to us, pushed on only by fear and caffeine. So, we pulled out the handsaws and rakes, setting to work on Bellevue Creek Canyon, removing pine needles and low branches along the way. Sure, we hoped it would help, but that unpredictable wall of fire kept telling us it was only a make work project – something to keep us occupied and sane while the flames advanced.

The next day the panic welled. Flames couldn't be seen in the daylight, but it was coming. As night fell, we stood on our deck and watched as the waves of fire crested ridge after ridge. I literally shook with fear and disbelief as we packed the remaining pictures and heirlooms. I kept saying that we didn't want to take everything because something may get broken. It would be a shame to lose one of those keepsakes needlessly. The irony.

We were packed and ready when our neighbour, Lori, came to the door. She had received word that flames had jumped the firebreak and were heading our way. We passed the message along to other neighbours, taking a few moments to watch its progress. Heading down the road, we had brave faces and optimistic words.

"We'll be back. They'll stop it…This is just a precaution."

In the wee hours of the night, after standing in line at the evacuation centre and driving to the home of our friends, Ron and Patricia, sleep finally forced me to stop watching the fire.

Morning came far too slowly. The start to this day promised hope. It was almost normal. Almost like we were visiting friends, having coffee on the balcony, but today we weren't watching the sun rise, we watched the smoke billow.

The generosity of our friends was tremendous. Despite their allergies, we were able to have our dogs with us. Our belongings were piled in various corners and the kitchen was open for food and comfort.

Hearing we were allowed back to our home for a couple of hours, the family headed to the evacuation centre. We waited in line to get our certificate proving residence, all the while commiserating with people we knew. Normally, getting through a public place with my father is difficult. But with a majority of the community wandering the town with no place to go, it took this gregarious teacher ages to talk to everyone. Yet these were the most important things that happened each day. The community embraced each other and truly rose to the challenge of supporting one another.

That afternoon, we went over to my brother's fiancée Taya's house and visited with her family, who welcomed us with space, laughter, compassion, and support. Later that evening as the sun slipped behind the mountain ridge, the glow of the fire attracted our attention. Our two families and some friends stood on the front lawn watching the candling of flames from where my family's community once stood. I will never forget standing with my father's arms wrapped around me, staring through misty eyes across the valley, watching as our home exploded and burned. Although no one told us that it was happening, we knew.

The valley has always spoken to me. It is my birthplace and it has a pulse that seeps through my blood. That night, it shuddered and I knew. There was no apology, only a pained twinge of remorse. Fire is a natural element, but that does not make it easy.

Suddenly, the radio announced there were more evacuations including our new "home" on the Rutland Bench. We moved quickly. Our hosts were at a local theatre production so we dashed back to their home. The whole group of us arrived at the house and began to load everything we could think of into the trailer. We were pretty efficient this time around and when our hosts arrived home, we had everything packed. Yet, when they arrived, disbelief set in. They did not think we needed to evacuate, but psychologically, my family needed to feel secure on the night we lost everything else.

Mom, Dad and I joined the rest of the family at Taya's home while our friends that hosted us stayed with the trailers for the night. On the deck, we talked into the wee hours with the television on in the background, hoping for any more information. Every new fact elicited a response from the group, whether surprise, anger, sympathy or rejoice.

The hours spent waiting were excruciating. The morning news came with estimates starting at 250 homes destroyed. I envisioned a decimated community. We lived on Bellevue Canyon, one of the first to be in the line of fire so we knew, but knew not. I watched the first airing of the media tour in our neighbourhood. I ask you to imagine whether or not you would recognize your own yard, one that you have spent countless hours creating and loving, without the house and maybe only a few singed shrubs. The first glimpse of the damage had me questioning, was that our house? And the realization came, it was. I called out to my family and we gathered grieving for what we had known for some time.

The following days were filled with meetings, confusion, tours of the community; things that were so emotive at the time, but have faded into the shadows of my memory. What I remember are the people. The friends and family who called every night, emailed every day and sat listening to the stories into the twilight hours. The sense of community that was emblazoned across our city was not superficial. It was a reminder of how much we care for one another, expressed in a time when our lives stood still long enough to listen. I now think that the connection I have always had to my valley is not only to the "natural" environment, but to the understated heart of the community.

There are days when I can't understand some of the things that happened. This wound has left a deep scarring on my sense of security, history, and family. I still feel like my past has been wiped off the Earth along with every ounce of safety. But I have gathered little miracles to my heart for comfort. Our childhood cups – found while clawing through the ashes looking for anything to salvage – have given me comfort. The fish in the pond who were fed by the utility men when no one else was allowed into the community, have given me hope for the little havens of protection found in the world. And the support of friends has enabled my family to cope and work together for our future. Now, as a family of adults, we have gathered one another into a bond that will prove to be more supportive than the one we had created as a family of children and parents. This bond has been created by mutual companionship, support, loss, and rebirth and will only grow stronger as we move forward.

Hope for Humankind
by Margaret, Michael, and Peter Kerr

Perhaps two days after evacuation we heard from a friend on the west side. "I think your place is still standing. I went down the lake a little way and had a good look, and I'm pretty sure your place is still there." What marvellous words to hear!

The following day, we went down the lake with him to have a look across. Sure enough, there it was! Through binoculars we could see our green roof and the reflection of the living room window. The house was still standing though all the land behind it was smoking, and also up either side of Cedar Creek. As we watched, a helicopter with its bucket made four or five trips down to the lake and back up to douse a smoking snag probably less than 100 metres from the house. What a heart-warming sight!

Upon our return nearly a week later, we discovered that ground crews had been in too, and had saved our home! The fire had gone around the yard on the east side. On the west, it had come up the bank and across the lawn. It had kissed the house against the concrete for a distance of about eight feet and had licked at trellises either side. There, the firefighters had stopped it! Though our outbuildings were gone, we could see the big wash marks from their hoses where the woodshed had been and also down the bank. Within a week of being back, the area where water had washed down the bank was flourishing with green grass shooting up. The subsequent rains also brought the lawns back to life, greener than they'd been all summer. Green was sprouting up everywhere from the nutritious ash, after a good downpour, and with no acidic pine needles smothering the ground any longer.

We were also most gratified to have had our neighbour at the winery put in a huge fireguard above us, going south from Cedar Creek. Also, at his lakeshore residence the fire was stopped from its northward advance up the lake from Bertram Creek, thus sparing our beach cottage. We also learned that our immediate beach neighbours to the south had a big pump and fire hose at the lake and had wet down our property before they left!

Our domestic water source is Cedar Creek and our holding tanks were extremely low as the creek had been dried up for some time. Skidders with water tanks on the back using our road to get up to hotspots, came up later and put several tank loads each of water into our holding tanks.

The gratitude one feels for the actions of neighbours and professionals alike, and for those who took us in, really makes one feel that there is hope for humankind, that when it comes to the crunch we are really one family. Many thanks to all!

Fires from Afar
by Danica Fruttarol

When lightning hit Squally Point, the feeling in my chest warned of the magnitude of the coming firestorm. From 300 to 1100 to 1800 hectares, the fire grew. No fire suppression at night brought fear into the deepest recesses of my brain. The instinct of impending danger. The taste of fear.

There was the naiveté of not knowing the scope of the danger. Common sense said it was okay. The fire would stop. The Okanagan Mountain Park Fire would burn itself out, away from the city of Kelowna. Thank goodness we had a wedding to plan.

Dana, my brother, and Lila got married two days after the fire started. Despite smoky air and the falling ash, the wedding dress stayed white. The ceremony was exquisite. Lila looked like the cover picture of a bridal magazine. The wedding went as planned and the bride and groom left for a honeymoon in B.C.'s backcountry, only to find it closed.

The newlyweds returned from their brief sojourn to await evacuation orders. They could protect their house and offer support to my parents. My parents, in their seventies, were pillars of strength and could offer their strength to Dana and Lila.

My parent's house was particularly vulnerable, situated next to the forest. Vera, a neighbour, thought she might take her grandchildren to a friend's house downtown....for a week's holiday. She thought the fire would surround Kettle Valley. She did not want to be in a big traffic jam trying to get away from the fire. Vera was right.

At night we watched the flames lick the sky. The spectacle from Kettle Valley after dark was astounding, the volatility of the fire in perfect view. Every hour or so one of us would wander from our beds into the street to see how far the fire had moved. The overwhelming fear staggered me several times. The fire was moving very aggressively. It looked like it would eventually encompass Kettle Valley. There were firemen and tourists and residents wandering the neighbourhood all night, watching and waiting.

The dawn brought forth more smoke and cinders and ash. You couldn't see the actual fire during the daylight, just a lot of smoke. The shorelines were edged with black soot. The insides of vehicles were dusted with ash. Carpets were blackened by footprints of soot. The construction continued in Kettle Valley, business as usual to an onlooker. It seemed surreal as the fire raged and the builders kept building in the path of the firestorm. Children played in the Kettle Valley Playground.

The winds brought chills to my spine despite the thirty-five degree heat. They fuelled unpredictable power into the fire . The shifting winds would redirect the fury many times: Naramata back to Kelowna. I was hoping Naramata would burn and how selfish that wish was. My family lives in Kettle Valley.

Four to five days after the lightning strike, I left Kelowna for my home in Eagle Bay. By then most of the Okanagan Mountain Park had burned. The realization regarding what items to take out of the houses entered the picture. Nothing. How could they choose what they wanted? Ray and Pat's forty-nine year marriage had provided them with an abundance of family treasures. How could they face the task of picking, choosing and packing certain items? One small box of "important papers" was all they needed.

Finally they decided to take a portrait of my sister Kim, now forty-five, that had been painted when Kim was around five years old. I thought of Mom's typewriter. Could you even buy one of those anymore? My daughter's bouquet she held at the wedding as bridesmaid. The turquoise vase. The orange stereo cabinet.

Pre-evacuation orders came just as I left. After leaving Kelowna the internet and media provided information for our family. We had all returned to our homes after the wedding... to safety. My mind tangled with the idea that we could experience a firestorm in Eagle Bay. I felt relieved to leave Kelowna but wanted to return to see what I could do. The best was to stay away. Kelowna residents needed all their own resources, not extra visitors.

Friday, August 22 the fire crossed Chute Lake Road. My sister relayed the information from Massachusetts that Quilchena was on fire. That is where my newlywed brother and wife live.

I had a shower, hysterically chanting, "the houses are burning. God pleeeease save the houses. Please let my family be all right." I was crying heavy tears.

The first sense of relief took me when my mother phoned. She asked me, "Are you all right?"

My dad was speaking in the background. "Tell her we're safe and that's all that matters." The strength of them crossed over to me. I was going to be all right as long as they were all right. They knew the fire could not really hurt them. All the people and the dog they loved were safe.

The firestorm has changed the people and the landscape. The forest is gone. The fire totalled my parent's fence and melted their garage door. Their landscaping is burnt. I marvel at the miracle that their house is still standing. The five houses across the street were levelled and the one beside theirs caught fire but was saved by firefighters from burning to the ground. The one adjacent was also damaged. Dana and Lila lost twenty-seven cedar trees and part of their sprinkler system also burnt. The Kettle Valley Playground, situated between the two properties, was completely burnt. These two families were out of their houses about two weeks.

Today most of the families are back in their rebuilt houses. A new beginning for these families. A time to reflect on the past summer and the miracle that no lives were lost due to the Okanagan Mountain Park Firestorm that could have taken the whole city.

A Staging Officer's Story
by Tim Light, Kelowna Fire Department

It seemed to be a summer not unlike most others I'd experienced over the years – wildfires are common occurrences in the news this time of year. I had no idea of what was just around the corner for us in this city, nor did I know how our city would deal with it.

We all heard about the lightning strike around Squally Point; we had concerns knowing how dry the forest was and how inaccessible the terrain was in that area, but it was still what we thought to be a long way from our town.

The four days leading up to Thursday were relatively uneventful for us as firefighters. It seemed we were in a wait, watch and see mode. Things were still in the hands of the Forestry people who seemed to be doing all they could to fight the "beast" as it became known in our Department. On Thursday evening that all changed. I was called in from home at 8 p.m. to cover for an officer who had gone out on our rescue boat. The rescue boat had been taken out to help with spotting the progress of the fire. I didn't know at the time but I wouldn't be home for three days.

Our job Thursday night was to protect the City of Kelowna in the downtown core and towards the Mission area as that fire hall was dealing with the fire in their area. I believe we lost 15 homes that evening in the Rimrock Road area of Kelowna but we saved 18. This fact does not make it any easier for those involved.

At 8 a.m. Friday my regular shift started. I work at our number one hall which is where our management staff work and where the EOC (Emergency Operations Centre) was being set up. You could feel it around the hall, people were on edge. Even with all that was happening in the Mission, we still had a city to protect so the guys on shift would deal with the day to day operations of protecting the rest of our city.

At some point, and don't ask me when, I was appointed staging officer along with Dave Leimert. Our job was to coordinate the equipment that would be assembling at our hall from all over our country. I had no idea of what we were in for. At one point of the fire, we had over 60 pieces of apparatus at our disposal and over 200 firefighters to organize. Another part of our job was to communicate with our fire ground commanders and find out what they needed, where they needed it, and then get it for them. The way it worked for us is when Dave was on shift I would be the staging officer and when I worked, Dave would be the staging officer. This would cover around the clock.

You see, in our line of work we all want to be hands on, so fighting the fire is the best place to be. Neither of us were terribly happy to be staging but we both accepted it as doing our part for our team. Friday evening is when, as it was described to me from some of our guys who were out there, the gates of hell opened up and swallowed over 200 houses in the city of Kelowna.

Listening to the radio that night at my desk, I could hear in the voices of my brothers (yes that's right, they're my brothers even if I don't know their names) the concern for themselves and for everyone involved. Imagine this, over 200 front line firefighters fighting the fire in the city and many more outside our limits and no serious injuries or deaths. When you think of it, it is quite miraculous. Over the next two weeks, we as a fire department were taken aback with the community and the corporate support we received.

From kids and families to the Pepsi and Coca Cola companies and many more, the support at that time was a huge part of why everyone involved could keep going out time after time. To this day we are still receiving support from our community. Now months have passed and people are rebuilding, the fire halls are back to their normal functions. By next summer we'll be saying that Kelowna has never looked better.

For those volunteers, army, forestry, and municipal firefighters from all over, we at the Kelowna Fire Department say thank you all for your great work. And to our wives and families who took care of our homes while we took care of others, we don't say it enough, but thank you.

FIRE STORM AND ME – THE DRY, HOT SUMMER OF 2003 BY NANCY WAGEMAN

a lightning strike... a mountain on fire...
my children are boated over with their 6 man crew... the 'sons of thunder,'
to dig guard, direct heli's, and climb;
in days they will be joined by 2,000 more... firefighters...

30 thousand people forced out by fire,
what do i take? i have an hour,
a picture, a tape-remembering my 'little' children's voices,
a favourite book and a coat.
will we get to come home?...
oh yes, we'll leave the goat.

grandparents, horses, dogs and cats too,
where do i take them?
i don't know, do you?
my heart's on its knees,
please help me think clearly, God, please.
thank you.

will bob be safe?
he's a firefighting volunteer...
i'll trust my family to my Father's care.
helicopters, planes, and police barricades...
my neighbourhood's changed...
are we playing charades?
no... bumper to bumper as i look from my car,
silent but deadly are the flames in the dark,
behind the mountain slithering over the top,
here comes the villain...
can we make him stop?

The Bubblegum House
by Lorraine Friesen

I remember the thunderstorm that brought the lightning strike causing the fire to start. I woke up to flashes of light, waiting to hear the rain on the roof that never came. Living on the edge of the forest had always had its risks and attractions. The possibility of a bush party campfire getting out of control kept us vigilant in the dry summer months. Therefore, it may have been a subconscious decision to take my family to the safest place possible during the third week of August.

Our family – consisting of my husband, our five and a half year-old daughter, our nine-month-old twins and myself – was looking forward to some well-earned family time. As we prepared to leave for holidays on Saturday August 16, we quickly organized a few items and brought them to a safe place, never seriously thinking the fire would reach our home as it was still 45 kilometres away. There was little reprieve from the nagging thoughts of what was happening back home.

The cell phone calls we received on Firestorm Friday from my brother and mother strongly indicated that if our house was still standing, we would be very fortunate. The fire had ripped through Kettle Valley and down our hill leaving charred and devastated ruins in its path. I had chosen vacation accommodations with no immediate access to a TV or a telephone. Snowy, fuzzy images on a portable TV only told half the story as we waited for news on our house, our family, friends, and neighbours. The next day we tuned into the news conference on the radio delivered by Fire Chief Zimmermann and other officials, broadcasting the addresses of homes that had been destroyed. We heard our address and our suspicions were confirmed.

Being away from Kelowna was both a blessing and a curse. We tried our best to laugh about it and to find an upside to this situation. We were totally helpless and I cried a lot. There were also an incredible assortment of feelings ranging from anger, guilt, confusion, and frustration, to relief and despair. Some words from our daughter put things in a clearer perspective. "Mom, everything you need is right here in this family. We'll all miss our house, but it's all just things. We have each other and all you need is in this family. We are all together."

For the sake of the kids and the fact that we believed our home was gone, we decided the best thing to do was to extend our "vacation" for a few extra days. We then returned to Kelowna to become evacuees. We heard rumours and unconfirmed reports that our house had somehow survived. The only way to know for certain was to take the bus tour arranged for people who had lost homes. As we turned the corner onto Chute Lake Crescent to drive down Curlew Drive, it was like entering a war zone. It was dark like a mid-winter afternoon, smoky with charred ruins everywhere where homes used to stand. It was heartbreaking to see our neighbourhood so totally devastated.

We saw that our house had survived the fire. In the confusion of figuring out damage, errors had been made with lot numbers and addresses. Two days later we were allowed to see the house and assess any damage. Our house had been heli-bucketed with fire retardant by the B.C. Forest Service, leaving a red sticky bubblegum-like coating all over. We could clearly see where fire had come within 10 feet of taking out our home. The smell, much like a burnt hot dog, and the stench from the fridge, was overwhelming, but to our amazement, the house was pretty much the same as we had left it.

Coming back home to stay was very difficult. Most of our neighbours were gone. Yellow caution tape and red and white danger signs were everywhere as were scorched and downed trees. Despite the fact that our house was okay, I carried a profound sadness and heartache for families who lost their homes and possessions. My mother had lost her home, which was quite close to ours, losing 65 years of keepsakes and belongings.

Even now, more than six months later, I still look out our window at the devastated forest and those feelings surface again. The reminders are constant and it feels as though our neighbourhood will never be the same. The hum and shriek of the huge logging machines and the rumble of logging trucks are part of the scenery up here.

For the Friesen family, the third week of August will always be remembered with an incredible range of emotions, a sense of awe at the power of nature, and a profound sense of gratitude. Our modest, little home surrounded by trees survived and so many others did not. Was it a miracle, dumb luck, or a firefighting strategy that saved our house? We may never know for certain. However, we are incredibly grateful for the efforts that kept our house intact and we thank those responsible.

Salt Spring Perspective

by Fire Chief Dave Enfield, Salt Spring Island

Like most of British Columbia, we watched with awe the affects of the fires in the interior during the summer of 2003. The Salt Spring Island Fire Department had filed with the office of the Fire Commissioner a list of equipment and personnel able to respond.

When the firestorm blew through, the news coverage was very comprehensive. Again we stared at our television sets as the fire laughed at all of the defenses the firefighters had put into place, pre-planning, fireguards, and back burns, hoping their efforts would not prove fruitless.

At 18:25 on Friday August 22, I received the phone call asking for our response. A couple of quick phone calls and I had five pre-arranged firefighters at the fire hall readying our apparatus. BC Ferries was contacted to ensure our priority loading; clothing and personal equipment were quickly gathered and it was home to say our goodbyes to our families.

As a 35 year veteran of the fire service, serving in Salmon Arm in 1998 during their fires, I was excited and nervous. What was I taking my guys to? Were they prepared? What were they thinking? Would we all come home safely? What would the personal effect on these firefighters be?

I had a mixed bag of firefighters responding: Capt. Dale Lundy with 12 years experience, Rick Kilbourn with eight years, Rob Grossman with three years experience including some wildland fire fighting in Alberta, and a young kid, Mike Bartle, with two years of limited knowledge.

I will always remember coming down the Kelowna connector. The night before had been very restless and I was dozing while Capt. Dale Lundy was driving. U2 was playing on the radio when Dale went "holy shit – look at that!" I awoke to see the plume of smoke and the blackened hillside across the lake.

After a quick check-in at Kelowna Fire Hall #1 we were dispatched to the staging area at Chute Lake and Lakeshore. We were assigned a young Kelowna firefighter to ride with us that first night and he tried to explain to us what we were going to see. As we entered the Okaview area I will always remember the five of us getting out of the two vehicles and staring at row upon row of chimneys, the total incineration of these structures; how plastic lawn furniture right beside this destruction was left unmarked, swimming pools looking invitingly clean, homes less than four metres away untouched.

We worked that Saturday evening from 17:00 till 08:00 the next morning. Everyone collapsed from complete exhaustion when we finally got to our accommodations at the university dorms.

Sleep came tough for some of us. Hot showers felt good but we were all restless. Four hours later we were up and ready to go again. Back to Hall #1 and back to the staging area by 14:00.

Sunday we worked with Lt. Shawn O'Reilly. This is one firefighter who truly wore his heart on his sleeve. He was devastated by what had happened, how all of their planning and efforts had not protected more homes. We worked in an area where their planning had paid off. They had cleared out a gully between two sets of homes, drenched the area with millions of gallons of water but the fire had still burnt through there. It hadn't touched any of the homes and they had been successful. He was proud, justifiably, of those efforts.

We toured an area off of Chute Lake Road that had a multitude of new homes. Right in the middle of these homes was a show home, advertising an open house that day. It was totally gone but the neighbouring homes, though suffering some heat damage, were intact.

We worked until 08:00 the next morning and tried to rest. The next two nights were spent in the Timberline area. We were sent to an area right at the end of the street where a large scale home was located. The fire, for some reason, burnt right up to the main building. It had destroyed numerous outbuildings but for some unknown reason, spared it.

I remember going down to the area right on the lake and viewing the destruction. As I was standing there a boat approached one of the private docks. I advised the lady and gentleman, both in their mid 50s, that they were not supposed to be there. They said they had to see their home. I escorted them up the walk to their house that was nextdoor and watched as the lady broke into tears. Everything was totally gone. The husband was upset as well. This had been their dream and it had been shattered. They had worked and toiled hard all their life, they told me, and it all went up in a puff of smoke and flames. They were going to rebuild and start their dream all over again.

When we departed Kelowna on August 28, we felt we had done a good job. We were totally amazed that no serious injuries had been suffered; we were embarrassed by all the pats on the backs, "Way to go guys," horns honking and people waving, no matter where we went. Two of us returned in September for a thank you party hosted in one of the subdivisions. We were royally treated and renewed some acquaintances we had developed during our brief stay.

The one major thing we all brought back with us was how all firefighters bonded together. No matter where you came from, whether you were a volunteer or career firefighter, you had a job to do and if you let differences get in the way you were detrimental to the main goal, to protect property and save lives.

We will never forget this experience.

Chapter Six
Joys and Sorrows

"The fire was definitely the scariest time of my life. It's hard for me now to even bring up those memories again because really when something like that happens it's in a different part of you: a part of your memory that you have buried and locked away."

HEATHER MATHESON

"Our hearts also go out to the families of the firefighters. They are giving up their loved ones to keep us safe, no matter what the outcome. I am truly sorry for the firefighters who lost their own homes trying to save others."

MAXINE DEHART

A WEDDING TO REMEMBER
BY MELISSA HARRIS (sister of the bride)

The date was set for August 23, 2003, a time of year when the sun is shining, skies are blue and the rain is minimal. On August 16, the bride drove into town with a list of numerous tasks to be completed for the week to come. She noticed the smoke billowing over a familiar park. Smoke in her wedding pictures, just what she needed.

AUGUST 17, her task on the never-ending list of things to do was to select the wedding wine, a trip to St. Hubertus winery with her mother and sister. The smoke in the air was evident, but the sweet taste of the wine masked the encroaching disaster. The wine was chosen and packed for the big day, but it was necessary for another trip to be made to the winery to pick up the wine glasses August 21.

AUGUST 18, the family was eagerly anticipating the rest of the families' arrival. Two homes were set aside for the visitors: one in South East Kelowna to house the groom's family and groomsmen; the other in Joe Rich, the location of the wedding ceremony, to board the bride's family. The Joe Rich house, due to the lack of rain, was running out of water in their well. Porta-potties were ordered to compensate for the lack of moisture, shower times limited to one minute in length and a waterbed bladder was filled at the South East Kelowna home and transported to the Joe Rich home to help support the dry well. The lack of water was not going to stop a wedding.

AUGUST 20, the fire was moving.

AUGUST 21, the wedding dress, mother of the bride's dress, and the maid of honour's dress were brought to Margo-Anne, a seamstress located on the south side of mission creek. The dresses were to be pressed and steamed and picked up the day of the wedding. The trip was made to St. Hubertus winery to pick up the wine glasses. Worries were obvious, yet the smiles and service were still outstanding and more so unbelievable. On the winery wall was a picture printed of the gates of St. Hubertus. It had been taken the previous evening with the fires off in the distance. The owners jokingly named the photograph the "gates to hell."

AUGUST 22 was the day of the rehearsal. Both homes were full and readily completing the necessary tasks the day before the wedding. The backyard of the Joe Rich home had been decorated. The wedding party arrived at the reception site at Eight Mile Ranch to decorate the barn only to find the horses removed for precautionary measures. But the party must go on, and the barn was transformed.

A mass of smoke that resembled a thundercloud was fast approaching. The marriage commissioner was to arrive at any given moment and the salmon was being prepared for the rehearsal dinner, but the commissioner had received false information of a fire on Black Mountain and had turned around at the top of the driveway. An uncle ran the rehearsal.

AT 7:00 P.M. the matron of honour received a phone call; her house in South East Kelowna was to be evacuated. She had ten minutes to remove her valuables. At 8:00 p.m. she and her husband arrived back at the rehearsal with their pets and photographs.

AT 10:00 P.M. the rehearsal was evacuated. Thirty-five friends and family loaded themselves into various vehicles and set off to find homes for the night. As the rain fell they realized that it was inevitable – the wedding could not be held in its original location.

The bride's family along with the groom made their way to a home in the High Road area. As soon as the family arrived, phone calls were made in hopes to find a new location for the wedding. The ceremony would now take place out at the family cabin, oddly enough, the location where the bride and groom first met. All who could be were contacted and informed of the relocation.

AUGUST 23, the big day and blue skies. It was time to quickly brainstorm and problem solve. The marriage commissioner and photographer were both contacted and confirmed their presence at the summer cabin on Kalamalka Lake. Eight Mile Ranch had not been evacuated and the food and décor could still be saved. A 8 a.m., the groom and a groomsman set forth to Eight Mile Ranch to pick up what they could. The groom, being a volunteer firefighter in Vancouver, was wearing his fireman's shirt, and managed to get through the roadblock on Hwy 33, also due in part to a sympathetic RCMP officer. He and his friend managed to remove all but the tables and table decorations from the ranch. They went directly to Kalamalka Lake. When they arrived, they couldn't believe their eyes. Twenty or more friends and family members had quickly transformed the rustic summer cabin into a little girl's dream come true. Borrowed tables were covered with white bed sheets, with wildflowers displayed in jars and china bowls. Borrowed lawn chairs were neatly arranged on the beach.

MEANWHILE IN KELOWNA, things were miraculously falling into place. The seamstress, although evacuated the night before, contacted the bride and informed her that she had relocated all of the dresses to a safe pick-up location. The flowers were in an area that was on evacuation alert, but those were retrieved as well. The DJ was able to relocate as well.

AT 2:00 P.M., the bride arrived at Kalamalka Lake and was in awe of what she saw: her aunts and uncles along with evacuated friends were busy running from cabin to cabin, barbeque to barbeque, cooking the roasts, hams and vegetables retrieved from Eight Mile Ranch. The cabin was completely transformed and was breathtakingly beautiful.

AT 3:00 P.M., the bride was carried by horse and buggy down to the beach to meet her groom, to be married at the place where they'd met, under the same blue, rainless sky.

For that one afternoon that led into an evening, loved ones were allowed to forget about the devastation only 50 kilometres away and took part in a day that would never be forgotten.

The groom returned shortly thereafter to continue fighting fires.

Take Our House if You Must

by Lee L. Nicholson

It was the thunder that woke me first. In the early hours of August 16, 2003, I looked out our windows that overlook the Okanagan Mountain Park and saw the trees silhouetted against a backdrop of a lightning lit sky. My first thought was how dry the park was. Unbeknownst to us, this marked the start of the Okanagan Mountain Park Fire.

We heard nothing of the fire until late Saturday morning when we returned home from shopping. Our son Courtney's friend Rob called to ask him about it. I phoned the Kamloops Fire Centre; they reported a small fire in the park, but had very little other information. Rob's mom rang later that afternoon and asked if we wanted to bring some of our belongings over to their place in Okaview; especially my husband's artwork. I assured her we were in no danger, but ironically, just a few hours later we were faced with that scenario.

Around 9:30 p.m., Courtney woke me. Our friend Don Miller from Glenmore was on the phone asking if we wanted his truck to move our things out. From his place, he was watching the "huge fire" over our way. Right after that other friends started calling, asking if we needed help or a place to stay. All of a sudden we realized the threat of the fire was very real.

There was a lot of traffic back and forth so I jumped in the car and drove through the park. There was nothing to see as we were situated too low. I returned home and as I pulled back into the driveway, a police car pulled in behind me. We were told to pack up what we could and to be out in one hour.

We phoned Don back, "Yes, please bring your truck." We began running up and down through the house. What did we need? Nothing seemed very important, a few photos… but mostly John's artwork. Things went into garbage bags; there was no time for suitcases. I opened my closet door, "No, I didn't need any of that." (The next day, I found I had only the clothes on my back).

The police returned not even 30 minutes later and said, "Get out now!"

Don wasn't allowed through the roadblock at Rimrock Road. My son and I and the dog piled into one vehicle, John followed in the other. We got to the roadblock to find Don waiting for us. I begged the officer to let us return with Don's truck to get the rest of John's artwork. They gave us five minutes. We raced back and the three of us were loading, sweating and shaking from exertion and shock. The police were back saying "OUT NOW!"

At the roadblock, people were milling around and lights were flashing. Vehicles were overloaded with belongings hanging off roofs of cars and out windows. I thought, "what will we do now?" Don did not hesitate and said "Of course, you'll come home with me!"

It was nearly midnight as we, a miserable and emotionally wrought bunch, started down Lakeshore Road. We stopped at Mission Hall, where I thought we had been told to register. We were greeted by loud music, people laughing and dancing; a wedding! It was surreal. Tears were running down my face. Courtney was stony faced in the car, the dog was jumping all over both of us, and our belongings were falling out as I tried to get back into the car; we were in shock.

After several stops to reorganize stuff falling off the roof, we finally arrived at Don's. Our minds were racing; no sleep would come. What's happening out there? The same question would go through our minds a million times over the coming weeks as we struggled to stay calm, positive and carry on with our lives as best we could.

On Monday, August 18, we were allowed home for a few hours. Everything looked normal; we were happy and relieved the fire had missed our neighbourhood. John wet down the house and yard with the garden hoses. Tuesday we did the same thing. I started to clean the house, wouldn't want those firefighters to have to use dirty bathrooms. And maybe I'd take my egg cup collection and my great grandmother's quilt. But the fire has passed us by!

Wednesday we were not allowed back out to the house. Fuelled by strong winds, the fire had jumped the guard and all of the neighbourhoods around us were being evacuated. That night we watched from Don's Glenmore home as the fire snaked up the mountain tops.

Meanwhile, our son Courtney had become terribly ill since the evacuation, unable to keep even water down. On Thursday as we moved to another friend's home, I could see the whites of his eyes looked yellow. We rushed him to Emergency at Kelowna General Hospital. That night around 2 a.m., as I was walked around Emergency sick with worry, I glanced up at the TV to see flames racing across the screen and heard the announcer saying, "Timberline." I went cold. Our neighbourhood! It didn't seem to matter though. I prayed, "Please God, take our house if you must, but don't take our son!"

The days were a blur as we moved automatically through each one. My lowest moment came when the meeting was called at Trinity Baptist Church regarding the loss of homes. We knew from the media that at least one of our neighbour's homes had been lost and that our neighbourhood had been ravaged by the fire. In desperation I phoned a neighbour at his hotel to see if he'd heard anything. We returned later to his message, "I have good news for you, your home is still there but the rest of our neighbourhood is gone." I called him back and we both cried for the loss, and for our neighbourhood.

Sunday, August 31, we were allowed to go home to assess the damage. It was a horrifying, despairing experience to see the blackened hillsides with ghosts of ancient trees. Rounding the corner to our street of five houses, we saw charred chimney stacks and yellow tape, then lastly, our home, standing alone in the hollow vegetation burned in a "horseshoe" from back to front, to within one metre!

As we opened the kitchen door, two items fell out onto the deck: one was a note from Captain Gerry Cadwalader and fire fighters Mike Jones and Troy Mullen of Victoria's View Royal Fire and Rescue, saying, "Quick... go buy a lotto!" The other was a cloth badge from the Comox Fire Fighters. They became known as "our firefighters" and we tracked them down to thank them personally.

As we had lost all our water lines, we had to haul water. But it was good to be home and to have one! We were happy to hear our neighbours were planning to rebuild. They said, "We will work together to make our neighbourhood beautiful again." We have set about doing just that! Our son recovered from his operation and returned home in mid-November. We are thankful that he is gradually regaining his health.

The Okanagan Mountain Park fire touched our lives in many ways, causing us to re-evaluate the importance of family and health over material things. The importance of friends and neighbours, and words of encouragement from complete strangers during that time were more than we'd ever expected in our entire lives! Good things came out of the ashes.

Great Angst from a Safe Distance

by Valerie Cottingham, Vancouver, B.C.

One of my dearest friends has lived for many years in a much-loved house on Curlew. There we have celebrated the ups and helped each other survive the downs of our lives on countless occasions. On July 25, 2003 she was married in her beautiful garden. I was in France and was only able to share this joyous day with her in spirit and on the end of a telephone line. Because of work commitments, I could not visit her upon my return and had to be satisfied with hearing the details in protracted calls and lengthy e-mails.

Then suddenly our interactions were all about the fire and I listened and read in disbelief as she, along with hundreds and then thousands of other residents of that beautiful valley gradually absorbed the enormity of the situation. On August 21, my husband travelled to Kelowna and sat with the newlyweds on their porch. They briefly toasted the marriage and he was given some wedding photographs to deliver to me. Then, of course, they talked only of the fire and their decision to wait it out in their home. Later that evening my husband heard the evacuation notice for that neighbourhood and was the one to call them to tell them to get out.

When he returned home the following day and I received the wedding photographs, I could not bear to open the envelope and see the innocent smiles. Again, isolated at the end of the phone line, all I could do was identify a temporary home for them with another friend and from there the calls between us continued. I heard the brave optimism fade and the fear escalate. We cried together when she called in the middle of the night: "I'm going to lose my home, Valerie ..." and I had to discipline myself not to call every few minutes to reassure myself that she was managing to cope at some level.

I would not presume to write one word about what went on for the evacuees and their community during the firestorm as I, along with countless impotent friends and family members, watched in horror from a safe distance.

As 1 p.m. on Sunday approached, minute by agonizing minute, I felt ill living the apprehension with my friend. I was prowling about the house by 5 a.m. and over the hours I made gallons of soup, spaghetti sauce and "Deb's Peach Chutney." What I thought I was preparing for I have no idea. I tried to be useful by calling any of my contacts in Kelowna who might be able to offer the family shelter on a long-term basis if their home was gone. How many such calls were made that day?

She called me as soon as she left the church but interference on the line overwhelmed her hysterical voice. I could just hear her yelling my name as I raced around the house trying to get away from the static - all the time yelling hers. Finally I was able to hear: "Valerie, I have my house, I have my house." Much out-of-control weeping followed.

When I hung up, my husband put his arms around me. "What are you DOING to yourself? This is not happening to you." I was confused. My fear, my grief, and now my joy were because it was all happening to her. How very odd to think that it could be any other way.

I walked downstairs, took the wedding photographs out of the envelope and looked at the smiles.

The Wedding Dress
by Rosemary S. Garner

It had been a perfect summer. We spent hour after hour playing at the beach with family and friends. The hot summer days slipped by effortlessly. This was the way summer was meant to be until the unavoidable happened and caught us naively by surprise.

We were camping outside of Vancouver when we heard the news of the fire. While our home was not in any immediate or even foreseeable danger, we decided we should be cautious and return to Kelowna. As we descended into the valley, we stared at the smoke-covered hillside in shock and awe.

Upon our arrival home, we cleaned up from our trip, deciding it would be best to air out the tent when the smoke had cleared. For the next two days we glued ourselves to the Castanet website, watching and analysing every new detail they released. We talked to family and friends, some of whom were in the forestry field and discussed the ever growing menace. Despite the advancing front and its potential trajectory, we reassured ourselves we were not at risk as we had not yet been put on alert. Other neighbourhoods much closer to the fire had been warned for days.

During this time, I began to feel increasingly uneasy about our situation and started to gather our family photos and a few needlepoint pictures my mom had made for us. On the second evening, my daughter and I went down into the basement to look for treasures too precious to lose.

Despite my heroic efforts over the years, our basement had a collection that could rival the Smithsonian Institute for volume. There were boxes of our children's school and art work, special clothes and keepsakes from their baby days, enough toys to open my own Toys 'R' Us and a large assortment of junk and family treasures. Faced with the overwhelming job of selecting specific items, while keeping in mind the limited volume of our vehicles, we began opening boxes and sifting through their contents. It was then that I came across a box which contained my wedding dress. Holding it, I remembered how my mother had wrapped it up so lovingly in special blue tissue and how carefully my father had labelled the box in his impeccable printing. My thoughts turned to my beautiful young 13-year-old daughter. She was like many young ladies of her age, anxious to establish her unique identity. I remembered how horrified she was when she discovered she actually looked like me. I laughed and showed her the box before putting it gently to the side. I assured her that I knew she would never want to wear it so we wouldn't worry about it.

As the next evening arrived, the sky cleared and a sense of relief filled the street. We stepped outside and surveyed the sunset with optimism. A while later, my husband announced it had been reported you could see the fire from Westridge Drive, a street near us. My heart froze. My husband and daughter went to verify this and when they returned fives minutes later, their faces told me what I didn't want to know. I had to go see things for myself and my daughter said she would come with me.

We ran a short way up the street to the canyon park where I felt we would get the best view. Seeing nothing, we stepped up on the split rail fence which marked the canyon hillside. At first it was quiet and dark. And then, out of nowhere, I saw the fire for the first time on top of the ridge. In disbelief I stared, watching as it advanced to distant trees with amazing speed. I was mesmerized and terrified. I noticed other neighbours emerging from their homes, anxious about the unfolding events.

The next few minutes were a blur of activity. We dashed home, helped throw what items we had gathered into our cars and locked up the house as though we were leaving on a trip. As we left, firemen and police were coming door to door asking people to leave as soon as possible. We were evacuated to my mother-in-law's home where we have been ever since, waiting for our new home to be built.

It was not until the following day when I went to unload the van that I found it. I lifted out the beautifully labelled box that held my wedding dress. As I stood there looking surprised and confused, my daughter smiled at me. She said that while she doubted she would ever wear it, she was sure it was too important to be left behind and that I would not want to lose it. I didn't know whether to laugh or cry. It was a moment my daughter touched my soul with her kindness. The worst was yet to come for us but it was one of those beautiful moments life throws at you in the midst of chaos.

Just Like Newlyweds

by Gwen Boek

While I am sitting here writing our story, Rusty, our 14 year old cat, jumps on my lap and tries to step on the keyboard, which does not make it easy for me to work. But I am so thankful we still have her.

I still remember the night we actually had to leave our home. I came out of a meeting at 8 p.m. and heard on the radio we were being evacuated. It was good the police were not doing any traffic control, because I am sure I drove almost 100 kilometres an hour to get back home, where I found my husband Adriaan on the roof with the sprinklers and the cat outside. She had not had her dinner yet so she came when I called her. Poor thing. She got shoved in the cat carrier.

Adriaan ripped the curtains from the window and threw them in the middle of the room, in case the window broke, the curtains would not catch fire. Smart thinking! We both looked at each other and without words, yanked my 100 year old grandfathers clock from the wall and shoved it in the van. Then the exodus began. That was the scariest part. Would we get down the hill safely? We did and finally arrived at our friends' house on Raymer Road beside the bird sanctuary. After just two hours, she was put on alert so we helped her pack. On Friday we all got evacuated and were welcomed in the house of another friend, where we stayed for 6 weeks.

When I think back on the days that followed the terrible news, it seems like a bad dream. I dreamt that I would wake up and find it had all just been a nightmare. But unfortunately, it was reality.

Since we have a store, people knew how to get hold of us and for weeks, even months, no day would go by that somebody wouldn't come to check on how we were doing. And not only that but the cards and gifts kept coming in. Even total strangers who had seen us on TV came with their wonderful tokens of love and caring. It was humbling to say the least. One lady brought us a basketful of typical Dutch items. Her mother had been a war bride and she wanted us to have these beautiful things. When she left the store Adriaan and I both cried. They all wanted to hear our story and by being able to talk about it, the healing started. A week after the fire, I broke down. I just wanted to go home, but there was no home anymore. And I cried and cried, until no tears were left. That was good.

Sylvia, our host, was wonderful to us, but we needed our own space. That was easier said than done. We have a cat and, oh boy, I do not know what people are afraid of. We finally found a basement suite where Rusty was welcome.

When we moved into our new "home," Rusty slipped outside and did not return. We were devastated. After everything we had gone through, this could not be happening. After nine days searching, advertising, you name it, I had given up hope. We drove back to the lot to see if she had returned home but we found nothing. And then one evening when I came home and called her again a small meow came out of the bushes and there she was, all skin and bones.

A month before the fire, our daughter Werna got married and we had fixed up the house and yard. It had never been so beautiful. We had a big party in the yard the evening before the wedding. Lots of family and friends were over from all around the world and stayed with us and with neighbours across the street (whose homes burned, too). After the fire disaster, these people wanted to do something for us; they had just been at our house and the memories were fresh and good. Well this is what happened: both our children and our new son-in-law live in Calgary and they had invited us to come and celebrate Christmas with them. We accepted this invitation but could not leave until Christmas day because of the store. When we arrived in Calgary that evening I noticed all the wrapped boxes under the tree. I thought this strange, since we've always kept Christmas moderate. After a wonderful dinner, we sat around the tree and learned all those gifts were for us. The children had set up a gift registry. They'd made a list of everything a person would need in their kitchen and also our Wedgewood dishes. Then they had e-mailed all these friends and family. I cried, it was so emotional but so fantastic. What a surprise! One of our old friends from Holland had sent a cheque to use towards replacing whatever we needed. We will use it towards the yard. Now we understood why they wanted us to take the van to Calgary. We felt like newlyweds. Unbelievable!

The year 2003 was the happiest and saddest year of our lives. We know 2004 will be good. We are going to have a wonderful new home again and even our first grandchild. We are so thankful for all our good friends that have been and still are here for us and also all the volunteers in Kelowna. We thank you all from the bottom of our hearts. The future looks bright again!

OUT OF THE ASHES (OF THE KELOWNA BC FIRESTORM, AUGUST 2003)
BY TESSA TESLUK

Listening to you and others...
Writing; Speaking; Emoting the same event.
New Words; New Perspectives; New Visions for me.

Viewing your art and others...
Painting; Photographing; Sculpting the same event.
New Mediums; New Perspectives; New Visions for me.

Welcoming your seeds and others...
Planting; Nurturing; Fertilizing memories of the same event.
New Ideas; New Perspectives; New Visions for me.

Flourishing with you, the forest and others...
Rebirth; Regrowth; Renewal from the same event.
New Life; New Perspectives; New Visions for me.

Dad, Mom, and King

by Wenda Pickles

This devastating wildfire began on my Mom-in-law's birthday, August 16, 2003. We had recently had to arrange for a care facility for Mom and Dad as Mom was terminally ill with cancer and Dad had dementia. We were able to get accommodation for both of them at Windsor Manor. We were travelling to Kelowna every week for three, four, and five day weekends. In other words, we were almost in Kelowna more than we were at our home in Surrey, B. C.

We heard about the lightning strike and fire in Okanagan Mountain Park at breakfast at our friend's house in the Mission. We did our errands and celebrated Mom's birthday and had dinner with other friends who live just off McCulloch Road. We left their place around 9:30 p.m. and we could see the flames from the end of their street. I became very anxious at seeing this. We carried on to our friend's where we were staying in the Mission and much to my horror, I could also see the flames from Gordon Drive. I announced to our friends how close it appeared and that I should help them to pack up some things just in case. They were confident the fire would never reach them.

On our return to Kelowna August 21, I was watching for the fire from the Okanagan Connector. I couldn't see anything but a large plume of smoke covering Kelowna. On crossing over the bridge, we were greeted with an eerie glow within a dense smoke fog. We could only see about a block ahead and in the headlights there were large and small pieces of soot and cinders falling from the sky. It was like being in the middle of a snow storm or how I would imagine a volcano eruption.

When we arrived at our friends' place near Gallagher's Canyon, the smoke began to lift, which meant a wind had come up. One of the neighbours called to say they could see the flames from their backyard so we went over to check it out. The soot and ash were falling on us and we were kidding around, brushing it off each other. In hindsight, this reminded me a lot of the boys kicking the ice around on the deck of the Titanic. We decided to drive a little further down McCulloch Road for a better look. We couldn't believe what we saw. We could hear sirens coming closer and closer then a long line of fire trucks screamed past us. Instant reality and terror set in over what was happening. We quickly returned home to learn that we were now on one hour evacuation alert. We immediately began packing up our friends' house. I have never in my entire life felt so insignificant and helpless against what was heading our way.

The next morning, still on one hour alert, we carried on with what we had to do and visited Mom and Dad at Windsor Manor. Mom and Dad were both wearing identification tags and wrist bands as they were also on one hour evacuation alert. We returned to our friends' house around 5 p.m. At 5:30 p.m. we received the dreaded news of having to evacuate as quickly as possible. It was overwhelming being so directly involved with such an experience. Of the three friends that we had been invited to spend our weekends with while caring for Mom and Dad, all were evacuated. When we came out of registration, the flames could be seen from the parking lot. We returned to Glenmore, our evacuation accommodation, via Dilworth Mountain and couldn't believe what we were witnessing. Sheer power – Mother Nature can be cruel.

It was an emotional rollercoaster for me. I was so worried about Mom and Dad. I was also panic stricken at the thought of our friends in potential danger of losing their houses and contents. Also, the reality of how many people were being affected in the same way and of course, the unfortunate families who had the devastating experience of actually having the fire consume their property. My heart just ached.

The following morning, August 23, we visited Mom and Dad and found that poor Mom had spent the night in the hallway on the main floor. She had a terrible night's sleep. There would have been no way to evacuate Mom if they lost power and couldn't use the elevators so all the second floor residents were moved downstairs. In the confusion, Mom lost her beloved constant companion, her praying teddy bear, King. After a couple of days, we found him tucked back in her arms where he belonged.

Mom and Dad survived the firestorm probably with less ado than most of the people but Mom lost her battle with cancer a month later. Dad joined her forty-seven hours later from what I figure was a broken heart. They are now together forever, all three of them: Dad, Mom, and King.

House of Dreams

by Dave, Jen, and Ella Rolleston

We started building our dream home on an acreage overlooking the lake beside Okanagan Mountain Park in February, 2003. It was our love for trees, the outdoors and Mother Nature that convinced us to place our home at the edge of a forest and inspired us to use salvaged wood to construct a large part of our home. Seventy year old timbers and flooring warmed the open design. Thought was put into the placement of each floor board and beam to show the character of the old mill in Squamish they had been reclaimed from.

While we built our beautiful home, we were pleasantly surprised to find out that my wife, Jen, was doing a little 'constructing' of her own. As the house began to take shape, so did her belly. Both the baby's due date and the house completion date were virtually the same time, mid August. On August 14, Jen's water broke while the last carpenter was doing his final touch-ups on the house. On August 15, after 12 hours of labour at the hospital, Ella Hope Rolleston arrived into our lives. Mom and baby were both healthy and happy and I was good until I cut the cord and well... never mind.

We arrived home to our brand new house with our fresh new baby. What a great feeling. Family arrived at the house to celebrate the baby's birth with a BBQ. At 7 p.m. the RCMP arrived at the front door. We were being evacuated. A lightning strike the night before had set Okanagan Mountain Park on fire and it was growing uncontrollably. The family packed up what was important (funny how many things you have in your home that are not really that important). We moved into Jen's parent's house for a few days until they also got evacuated. We then moved across the lake and stayed with some close friends.

That night, we watched our house burn down through a telescope. Talk about closure. After three weeks the fire had finally subsided and it was time to start thinking about what to do next.

We bought our builder's show home partially furnished and moved right in. We are calling this home for the next year or so. Our property looks quite good but we want to see how the grass and trees look after the spring before we make the decision to rebuild.

Ella has now doubled her weight. She laughs all the time… mostly at her father trying to make weird noises. Our friends' and family's support enabled us to stand strong and overcome what was both an exciting yet extremely challenging year. Mother Nature took away our home and gave us a joyous baby girl in return. We couldn't be luckier.

Rest Home Evacuation
by Linda Shaw

I cringed when I heard about a small fire on the east side of Okanagan Lake. I just knew it was no little fire.

The closer it came the more nervous I became. When it peaked the ridge, claimed its first home and back-tracked, I still could not settle. I knew it would return – and with a vengeance! I felt somewhat safe until I actually saw the flames from my front door. I then became anxious about my disabled husband and the seniors at Sutherland Hills Rest Home where I work as an LPN and HCA.

The daily questions became, "Will we have to leave?" and, "Where will we go?" We knew we were in a danger zone because of our beautiful trees and Sutherland Park across the street. Suddenly, pine trees did not possess the same beauty. We began to hear horrific stories about fireballs claiming dozens of homes. When my husband told me we were on alert I started to pack my most treasured items. He soon joined me packing his valuables and our daughter took them to Winfield for safekeeping. We packed pictures, tools, china, and barrels and bins of things I inherited from my mother – things that had displayed her inner beauty that could not be replaced.

At the rest home we kept the windows closed, wore smiles, hugged, and did everything to keep peace and calm. We had daily briefings about the possibility of a move and then the dreaded day came.

It was supper time and we were instructed to feed the residents as usual and then move them to the lounge in preparation for evacuation. Then we were told to resume normal activities as our evacuation location was also unsafe so they had to find us another place. We remained calm and worked well together comforting ourselves, the residents, and concerned family members.

I feared for my disabled husband when I was unable to reach him by telephone. My daughter came immediately from Winfield and rescued him and our camper full of things we treasured. My husband was terrified as he could hear the roar of the fire from our front door.

Sutherland Hills filled up with volunteers, concerned family members, and staff. All were put to work marking beds, checking rooms and moving people to the main evacuation area on the west. When everything was seemingly ready I went from room to room checking to see if all the beds had been properly marked and clothing was included according to our evacuation instructions. I also tucked their bibles inside their beds and special stuffed toys were tucked inside pillows so they would have a means of comfort in their temporary home. I could see the flames clearly from Hall and KLO Roads and felt devastated.

We evacuated to Vernon, arrived, and were lost. We stopped at an ambulance hall and they received permission to lead us directly to our destination. When we arrived we were told to go to a second location, Nordic House, and the ambulance attendants graciously escorted us there, where I remained for the duration of the evacuation.

Privacy and having only two bathrooms in the common room were our greatest challenges. We used blankets, sheets or whatever we could find to provide curtains. Sometimes we used our bodies as shields for privacy. We comforted, laughed and assisted each other with specific routines. The staff of Nordic House was superb and I loved them dearly. They were always visible, near at hand and willing to do whatever they could.

We remained in Vernon six days and then returned. I was anxiously waiting for the residents at the entrance of Sutherland Hills, tears in my eyes, as they came through the doors. To some, it was a nightmare, others, a holiday, and others – a trip from danger to safety. They were so happy to be home again; back in their own rooms with their girls and guys to care for them. Some, remembering my name, came to visit and thank me for caring for them in Vernon. Others reached out to me or hugged me in acknowledgement.

Carl Denis, our 99-year-old resident, and Mr. and Mrs. Wirtz, had refused to evacuate. I worried, as I love them dearly. Carl couldn't stop hugging me! He said I was the first woman he'd seen in days and what a welcome sight I was. He couldn't stop talking, wanting to know everything about everybody.

My husband and I were on alert a second time so our grandchildren and daughter came to the rescue again. It took until Christmas to unpack from our second evacuation. I am grateful I was spared great loss and I still have the tangible items that rekindle memories so precious to me. The fire will never be forgotten – nor will the closeness that developed during that time between families, friends, residents, and staff. We too are heroes – all of us who have survived such a traumatic time.

Chapter Seven
Miracles and Memories

"As we were sitting there trying to get into the long line of cars, the miracle happened. It's the thing I'll remember the most about the night of the firestorm. Rain started falling, and it came down hard. As it did, cheers erupted from the long line of vehicles."

SHARON WEBER

FIREFIGHTERS...
You tried your best
and we thank you!
Doug, Jan, David & Jason Amundrud

"Spoke to a man involved and asked him to describe how a fire burning so hot and deep could suddenly change direction, from moving east to moving south. He said it was a miracle and tied it to the faith of the people at Mountain Home. The fire stopped before their dwelling. In changing direction, all the houses in June Springs were spared, for which we're eternally grateful."

KAREN VINGE

REMEMBERING OKAVIEW
BY ALISON BOOTH MCNAMAR

Twenty years ago, Okaview was just like **any other road you'd find on a map,** but to me it was the centre of the universe. Back then, this new development was chockful of young families, building their homes amidst the beautiful forest overlooking Okanagan Lake. We were among some of the first children to live on that street, back when Peach Flats was a blanket of trees, just waiting to be discovered.

My brother and I knew our little corner of the world like the back of our hands. Every family, every landmark, every detail. We knew the best places to toboggan, which family kept their pool the warmest, and whose Mom bought the best cereal. Sleepovers and pool parties were a regular occurrence, as was showing up at the last minute with three extra kids at lunchtime. Being gone for hours at a time was normal. Doors were left unlocked, and we always felt safe. Our parents rarely worried about us, for there was an unspoken trust between the families on our street. We were not just neighbours; we were friends.

For many kids in the Upper Mission, the forest was our playground. Because we lived a fair distance from the nearest park or beach, we spent a lot of time in the woods exploring, building tree forts, constructing bike jumps, and playing hide and seek in the dappled sunlight… our voices echoing off the firs and the pines.

During the summer, we would play until it got dark, knowing it was time to start heading back when the sky turned pink over the lake and the trees became familiar silhouettes. I remember countless times walking up that hill at the hush of dusk, making our way to our homes. Homes that are no longer there.

The decision to go back was a difficult one for me. After returning to the Mission to raise my own family, I often drove up to the old neighbourhood showing my kids where I grew up and the places I played. I had just taken them there a few days before it was evacuated, and could not believe it when the news came that it was gone. After spending more than half of my life in that area, I had to see if it was true. And tragically, it was.

As I stood and stared out in disbelief at my childhood street, all I saw was driveways and swimming pools, ashes and rubble. My brain searched for old landmarks, those familiarities of home, but my eyes saw nothing but devastation. Chimneys were lined up, one after another, like grave markers on our childhoods. And the trees were stripped black and jagged, like something from a horror film. I was in a state of visual shock.

The house I grew up in was gone. The home my Mom painstakingly designed for us 23 years ago had been reduced to nothing. Our front path led to nowhere. And even though my parents no longer lived there, the heartache was still overwhelming. Heartache for the new owners, and heartache for all our friends who still lived in this neighbourhood and lost everything.

As I walked down the street in the early morning light, I made silent wishes of comfort to both friends and strangers. I was overjoyed to see the houses that were spared, and the trees that survived. I was so happy for the families who still had homes, and so thankful to the firefighters who fought courageously to save them.

My mind wandered along with my feet, then began to flood with memories. Everywhere I looked I was bombarded with mental snapshots of my life. The spot where I rode my bike for the first time without training wheels, the driveway where my friend got bitten by a dog, and the curb I used to sit on and watch my brother play street hockey. I gazed up at the charred hillside where we used to ride our crazy carpets, then down to our old bus stop, and further below to my swimming pool where we all swam, covered in red dots the summer the whole gang got chickenpox. My brain felt like it was going to burst.

When I reached the end of my walk, I could barely move. My limbs were heavy like cement, yet I was light-headed. It was all too much to comprehend. I thought that maybe I shouldn't have come so soon, that maybe I wasn't ready. Then I sat down on Okaview Road and I cried.

After a few minutes, a flash of colour caught my eye amidst the grey landscape. Flowers were still growing where an old friend's house used to stand. I smiled, thinking how even though they were a small miracle, they were a miracle nonetheless. Those yellow blooms reminded me of each member of that family; amidst all this destruction, they had survived. And that was the true miracle.

As I got up to leave, I felt a strange sense of solace. I was so grateful to still have my memories, and know that the people I made them with were not harmed. I realized that these kinds of reminiscences weren't flammable, and aren't stored in a cardboard box. They are embedded in your soul, no matter where you call home, and nothing can take them away.

My brother and I had an amazing childhood in this community. We were so fortunate to have grown up here, and so blessed to have spent time with the many great families who called, and still call Kelowna their home. And I know that in the not so distant future, these fire ravaged streets will get back to being the centre of the universe to the next generation of children who live here, just like Okaview Road was to me.

Modern Day Miracles

by Lee Gibson

The week was like a pendulum. One day I felt nervous and frightened as choppers and water bombers roared overhead, like I was living in the TV show M*A*S*H. The next day I'd become complacent as the fire seemed to head in a different direction. But Monday night was frightening. I could see the flames at the top of the hill above my home. We went on evacuation alert that night. Tuesday I phoned my friend Glenda because I knew she had a furnished house to rent. I said, "I hope I never need that house but if I do, is it still available?"

Little did I know that in three days I'd be homeless. Why did I make that call? It's not that I'm so smart. Our house hadn't even burned down yet. But I think God was looking after me. That's a modern day miracle.

Just after the fire, a song was sung in church. It was like the lyrics had been written for me. "I will never be the same again. I will never return, I've closed the door." Profound words. Our life would never be the same again. Literally, we could never go home. We had closed the door for the last time on August 21. Our joys and memories would have to be enough.

It was difficult telling my 88 year-old mother that the home she and my dad had built 33 years ago had burned to the ground. My son was 17 years old when our house burnt down. When my mom's son was 17, he died of encephalitis. Her loss was in a totally different category than mine. That comparison helped me keep things in perspective. This was not the end of the world.

Has any good come from this? Firstly, I am learning to keep my priorities straight. The most important things are really not things. Good health, safety, family, freedom – I have these to be thankful for. Compared to about 75% of the people in the world, we are much more fortunate.

When we left our home it was about 35°C so I wasn't too well prepared for the cold days of winter ahead. But when a friend called and offered me some of her clothes, I was totally embarrassed. Me? Take her clothes? How could I? After all, I'm the one who likes to give, not take. This was so out of character for me. At first I totally ignored her offer. I didn't want handouts. But in retrospect I realized I couldn't be proud. I actually needed almost everything. How humbling to have so little and yet be ashamed to take anything from someone else. Is there a lesson here for me? I've always been sensible and prepared for the future. But a house fire doesn't fit into anyone's plan. None of us left our homes expecting never to return. We all thought we were going home again and this event was a mere inconvenience for which we were taking precautions. But now I'm vulnerable. I'm not self-sufficient and I have to be receptive to others who want to help me. I am learning to graciously say, "Thank-you!"

One day I picked up my daughter Sheena from school and she said, "Mom I got a shoebox today. I never thought I'd *get* a shoebox!" A high school in Vancouver had sent a shoebox filled with toiletries, movie rental vouchers, etc., to each teenager who'd lost his or her home. It was awesome. Not just for her, but also for the students who had given their time, money, and effort to put them together.

Now that we're living on the Westside, my children drive to school together every day rather than take the school bus. One day I said, "You can leave here about the same time as you used to and get to school on time. It isn't that bad." And Scott, who is in grade 12, said, "Not that bad? It's great. I get to drive to school and not take the bus."

Scott and Sheena are spending time together that they never would have otherwise. As a result, I see a change in their relationship. They are getting to know each other better through those drives back and forth to school.

Did I do everything right when I left my home? No. I could have done some things differently. And I know everyone has his/her own way of dealing with life's hurdles. We have unique personalities and other factors influencing our lives.

But I'm not wasting my time with regrets. Actually, I don't have time. I had to list every item that was in my house. Then price it. That's what those of us who lost our homes have been doing. At the same time, we're replacing the necessities. And we're planning a new house. Building a house is something my husband Jack and I had never even considered. Now we have no choice. You could call it a major inconvenience. The rest of our lives are on hold as we piece together what remains from the fire and try to move on.

A few months after the fire Sheena said to me, "We don't really have miracles like in the olden days when God sent manna from heaven, do we?" I said, "Maybe the miracles aren't so obvious, but for me to call Glenda and ask for her house was a modern day miracle."

Lost Treasures
by Pam Horak

Most of the people who were evacuated due to the Okanagan Mountain Park Fire left behind many of their treasured keepsakes: some due to lack of packing time, others due to no way to transport them, and some were simply forgotten in the rush. Those of us able to return to an intact home were lucky indeed. I remembered some important items I should have taken with me only after I was evacuated. Those things were still there for me when I returned. The unfortunate individuals with no home to return to lost many irreplaceable items. One man commented that it was painful to look at the wreckage of his newly completed house; he wanted it removed as soon as possible.

Being one of the companies doing clean-up of the burned homes, some of the owners asked us to watch for certain items they hoped might have survived. As the work progressed, most houses were so completely burned that nothing remained. We scooped rubble out of basement after basement that consisted of nothing but ashes and cement.

There were sometimes strange things that were recognizable but totally unusable. I saw cement logs from a gas fireplace – no fireplace, just the logs. I saw the shape of a boat trailer with a burned engine sitting on it; the hulk of what had been someone's exercise equipment. Lots of patios had bent metal frames that had once been attractive lawn furniture. One had a garden swing frame still sitting there looking out at what had been a lovely view of the lake, surrounded by large pine trees. The view was now a sweeping vista of charred trees and rocky terrain. Many a yard had buckled up remains of metal garden sheds and burned off garden hoses with a burned sprinkler on the end, left to water down trees and bushes in a fruitless effort to hold back the fire.

One morning a month or so after the fire, Joe, the excavator operator, was starting yet another demolition of a burned home. As he was digging into the charred pile that he was loading onto the trucks, something caught his eye. It was some paper and books. He climbed down out of his machine to take a closer look, walked around to the front of the machine and started picking through the refuse. He thought, "Someone is going to want this!" It was just at this time that the homeowner drove up to watch the procedure. Joe called the lady over to have a look, she couldn't believe her eyes – there were her children's pictures taken at some long ago birthday party! They had somehow survived, albeit a little singed, along with the negatives. The lady then burst into tears at the sight of what she had thought was surely gone forever.

After so many sad events it was nice to be able to report some small happy one.

A Time to Remember
by Elizabeth Roszak, Montreal

It was the evening of Thursday, August 21, 2003 and I had just finished speaking to a very close friend of mine in Peachland, when I decided to go online and listen to Sun FM. "We are interrupting regular programming..." were the first words I heard. What followed next became frightening, over-whelming, and almost impossible to comprehend. The announcer began to report that the Okanagan Mountain Park Fire was raging out of control and had broken through the firebreak at Rimrock Court. Crews from near and far were doing their best to try and contain those flames along the perimeters that were still accessible and had a better chance of being managed. There were reports where flames were seen to soar over 100 metres into the night sky. I sat there with bated breath, trembling, and listened as evacuation alerts rapidly changed to evacuation orders for thousands of Kelowna residents. People were being told "not to panic and to leave the specified areas in an orderly fashion." They were asked to leave their lives behind, to walk away into the unknown, wondering what fate would befall them in the aftermath.

Minutes turned to hours as I kept hearing familiar streets like Bellevue Creek, Raymer Road, Crawford Road, June Springs Road, McCulloch, etc., being read off like kids' names during roll-call in class. Fear took over my sense of security. I can't remember now if the alerts for Springfield, Hollywood, Ziprick, parts of Highway 33 and others were issued on the Friday or the Saturday during the continuous coverage on Silk FM and on Castanet. One day seemed to flow into the next. All I could think about was, "How much longer?" I remember hearing that a long-term care facility for the elderly close to Kelowna General Hospital had been evacuated... I thought to myself, "My God, please, not the hospital." The heartbreaking recollection of going back and forth with my father from Rutland to the Cancer Centre on a daily basis for radiation therapy two years earlier became so ominously vivid. At 81, my father disliked taking the highway. The various roads, streets and avenues would likely be at an even greater risk by the fierce, relentless and formidable foe if not for the strength and willingness of a community that came together so wonderfully well! I have lived in Montreal my entire life, except for a brief period in time (during five months in 2001), when I called Kelowna my home. Physically, I was over 5000 kilometres away and nowhere near any of the fires. But believe me when I tell you that my heart and my soul were right in the thick of it.

For days on end I kept up with the continuous live coverage online along with the CBC News bulletins and special reports on TV. Also, with the help of my good friend in Peachland who gave me his perspective on what he saw from across the lake, I was able at least to try and understand some of what was going on. I didn't smell the stifling smoke, I didn't feel the hazardous heat, and I didn't see the flagrant flames. But I do know about loss and what it feels like. I also saw and heard about how an amazing group of people within a community withstood the test. You fought an uphill battle and won! Be proud in knowing what you accomplished by showing the rest of the world "The Little Town that Could." In closing, I just want to say that a very, very large part of my heart will forever remain in Kelowna.

Oh, Christmas Tree

by Lynda McGowan

Visiting friends in the Kettle Valley area, I commented on how close the helicopters seemed to be. It was only a few minutes later that we saw the flames dance their way over the ridge. It is difficult to express the feeling of terror when you finally realize how close you are to something so wild and uncontrollable.

We had been watching the ash fall on our back deck for the past week. We trusted that the "powers that be" had everything under control and that we didn't have to worry about it reaching our home. We had purchased this home a year and a half ago with the intention of living the rest of our lives here. My husband Bob told people, "They will have to carry me out feet first to get me to leave this home." A Kelowna builder had built this home for himself and his family and lived in it over ten years before selling it to my husband and me. We recognized that it was a well built home that afforded us the luxury of having what we needed on the main floor plus plenty of room downstairs for when the family visited.

As we ran home from Kettle Valley to our house on Curlew (only a couple of blocks away), a state of panic was setting in. What do you take at the last minute that will fit into two small vehicles? As I ran through the house collecting pictures and other odds and ends, I asked my husband to grab the hard drive. He was busy putting our two old (and nothing special) bikes on the new bike rack we had purchased the day before. Next thing I know, someone is at our door telling us we must move along and get out. Where was Bob? He was down in the lower level looking for a ski helmet. He suggested I go ahead in my car - no way! I would have gone crazy worrying about him still looking for things at the house. I insisted he get in his car and lead the way out of the neighbourhood.

We headed out only to be caught up in traffic on the section of Curlew between Lark and Chute Lake road. We could see the flames coming down the mountain near Kettle Valley but we couldn't move. Cars were coming from other areas and we were stranded for almost an hour. We phoned our children and kept them posted. Finally the RCMP arrived and began directing traffic so we could all get down the hill.

This occurred Thursday evening. Friday we lost our home to the Okanagan Mountain Fire. Saturday evening we were visiting in the home of a local firefighter, just a couple of doors down from my daughter's home where we were staying. When he came in, he told us he had been working in our area. We showed him where our home was on a map he had. He had just come from there and was sure our house was gone. I refused to believe this. When I went back to my daughter's I had a good cry and hoped that when we attended the meeting at the church the next day, we would find out that he was wrong. Unfortunately, he was right. That same evening we saw what was left of our home on the national news.

We were in shock for some time. As the Christmas season approached, we realized we had lost not only our Christmas decorations, but also my daughter's and her mother-in-law's decorations. Our decorations were special as many were artistic efforts created by our four children over the years. It just didn't feel right to go to a store and replace them with new decorations. That's when I came up with the idea of having a Christmas Open House, with the price of admission being a Christmas decoration that preferably came from their personal collection. When the day came, we were more than pleased at the generosity and creativity of our friends. We received decorations that were handcrafted, decorations their children had made, some they had had for the duration of their married lives. We tagged each decoration with the friend's name and let them place it on our (Charlie Brown) Christmas tree. Next year, when we unpack the decorations for our tree, they will all have special meaning (as Christmas decorations usually do). We will be able to decorate our tree in our new home and be reminded of the kindness and friendship we had in our lives in our time of need.

Vera's Hat and Scarf

by Shirley Anderson

It was October before our Kettle Valley Walking Group decided to try and find our trails through the woods south of the town site. We wondered how it would feel, walking through the burnt forest. Nothing looked familiar. The woods were empty of growth; stark and depressing. All that remained was the black bones of the trees. The trail was still there so we continued on. After a climb, there is a spot that overlooks Cedar Creek where we stop for a break. This is where we observe the activities of a family of ospreys each spring. Lo and behold, away up high and across the deep ravine, we could see the osprey's nest was still there. While looking around at the tall pines, burnt black by the fire, imagine our delight to see the young fir tree we decorate each Christmas still standing and still green.

Further along, we climbed what had been a very pretty little knoll. Everything was charred and black. All the trees and shrubs were gone. This was where another tree stood that we used to decorate, but all that was left was a black skeleton. It had been a beautiful, bushy pine. Everyone was expressing sad "ohs" and "ahs," except Vera. What she said was, "It looks so sad. It needs a hat and scarf." A couple of weeks later we hiked the same trail and when we arrived at the knoll, Vera decorated that black skeleton with a brightly coloured hat and scarf she had knit just for our poor little Christmas Tree.

Divine Inspiration

by Rob Wilkinson

I live in the middle of Rutland, an area surrounded by a concrete jungle, not even near any danger of this firestorm reaching our home.

The day after the August 2003 firestorm started, I had a dream. At 2 a.m. I was suddenly awakened by an incredible picture of a three-dimensional crystal fireman's helmet. I sat up in bed and started to draw this dream. That following day I told my wife Linda what I had seen in this dream. She ventured a quick unrelated remark, as she was looking out over our balcony and talking about what we need to pack. I could see tension and panic in her eyes; they were as wide as saucers.

Three days later, as we were watching the beast crest over the second south ridge, we started getting panicky type phone calls from my family in Edmonton, very concerned for our safety. We told them we were on the standby evacuation list.

Every day the blaze got bigger and so did this dream; it literally consumed my total thinking. I started to draw more and more pictures of this dream. I collected every news clipping I could get my hands on. My wife Linda thought I was losing all my marbles. Bless her for her patience and understanding. I was in a state of obsession, yet I consider myself quite a stable and rationally sound person. So why the obsessive behaviour about this dream? (I must add that I do not remember many of my dreams but this one was so clear).

After the fire had been put out in the suburbs of Kelowna and life seemed to be getting back to a normal pace, I quickly started my research on the internet and went into my own world consumed by this fire. The passion that put me on this path was not known at this time. The more searching I did, the more muddy this dream became. Why, why, why? That's just great, I thought to myself, feeling frustrated and disappointed. I was getting so intolerable that I couldn't even stand to be with myself.

Bless my wife for her undying grace, patience, and love for me. She is my partner and I bounce a lot of stuff off her. She usually has good sound judgment on most things – a Type "A" personality who likes all her ducks in a row before anything is started (she has a yellow duck on top of her computer and it watches me all the time). I must be type "R" for rabbit trails.

While searching on the internet, for what, I'm not sure, it hit me like the backhand I used to get when I talked back to my parents in the good old days. Never before have I attempted to do this but I knew if didn't try, I wouldn't know. "God you want me to do what?" I felt like Noah building a boat in the middle of the dessert.

OK God! I'm humble, what is it you want from me? "Sculpt a fireman out of clay."

I'm in my mid 40s and maybe my hearing is starting to go so I asked, "Sir, did you say scrap the fireman and pray?" I'm sure Noah had a few choice words with God at the time of the flood. I too had some choice words, like why? Give me a pencil, I'll draw; give me some paint, I'll paint; give me a digital camera, I'll shoot, that would be the easiest.

The vision/dream I had is crystal clear now and it has changed my life by God's grace. The first bronze covered sculpture titled "Heroes in the Line of Fire" was displayed at the Kelowna Art Gallery in the month of February. Signed and numbered edition sculptures are available to commemorate the firestorm and thank some of the many who worked so unselfishly to protect our city. I pray that God restores back the great losses of the people directly affected by last year's firestorm. Amen.

Never Imagined
by Jorie Soames

I never imagined the noise of helicopters and water bombers flying right over my house from sun up to sun down would be a comforting sound. Neither did I believe the fire would devour its way into residential Kelowna. Certainly we would douse it once the terrain wasn't so steep, once we had broad streets as natural fireguards and hundreds of personnel and machinery on the job. No fire of any magnitude would dare to enter our fair city. Wrong! Lesson one: Fire does not submit to my thoughts.

I live on the Belgo Bench, towards the north-eastern corner of Kelowna. The area features orchards and vineyards and open land that gently rolls.

Our involvement with the fire started early on with my husband's call to fire duty, running heavy equipment. This meant he worked through the nights, coming home black and tired for sleep and food, then back to the fire. He had been called to fire duty before, but this time seemed different. I was up at odd hours, sleeplessly pacing and fervently praying for the safety of people on the front lines. He said things would be OK. The fire could be stopped. As night after night went by, I saw another message in his eyes. I also saw less and less of him as he was called more and more.

My life suddenly shrank to taking care of our three little ones, trapped in a house without any fresh air: a trying experience for even this seasoned mom. We made the best of it. We listened to the radio and put our name in to take billets. My eight-year-old son would phone the guys at CKOV and they would put him on-air to have a little chat. He would send news of his dad's progress over the airwaves and beseech Kelowna to pray for the firefighters. The guys at the station loved him and seemed to know that Reuben called because he missed his dad and needed to talk to some men who knew about the fire.

Friends were evacuated and phoned to say they were on their way. Turning down bed sheets in the guest room gave me a feeling of finally doing something to help. It brought back strong memories of the night our house burned eight years ago. Fleeing with few possessions. Sleeping in strange beds. Relying, worrying, and feeling numb.

The phone disturbed my thoughts.
"This is Shelley, I think your road is on the alert list."

"No, I don't think so, we're quite far from the fire."

Shelley wasn't the only one to call. Within the hour it was confirmed by more phone calls and a look at the TV. There, in full colour, Kelowna was staging a warped version of the *Three Little Pigs*, the big bad wolf huffing and puffing in hot pursuit, threatening to blow all the houses down.

The Jansen family came immediately to help me pack and get my husband's artwork out safely. Some of Tom's early works had been destroyed in our first fire so I was determined not to let that happen again. The evacuation order came within hours. Police drove up and down the street, their bullhorn voices carried on the wind like sounds from a far off stadium on a summer night.

Our expected guests drove on by. At some point hubby showed up tired and dirty – sent home to evacuate. No fighting the friggin' inferno that night, no matter how big your bulldozer. The guys climbed on the roof, wind blowing forcefully. The fire was coming hard and fast in the form of an orange-red ball travelling directly towards Rutland.

Children were loaded into the Jansen's vehicles. Watching them flee into the night felt like a scene from the London blitz, mothers putting their children on ships and sending them off to safety. "Please don't let the ship sink."

Neighbours called for pets and loaded what livestock they could. Cat into a laundry basket; Nigel the rabbit in her cage into the truck; bicycles thrown on top to weigh it all down. Last minute items in hand, I came out the door just as lightning lit up the sky, rain pouring onto my face. A miracle? Probably. I took it as back-up to my husband's mutterings. "Hurry up woman, its time to go."

As if on cue, car doors shut, motors started up and a stream of cars, trucks and campers left Belgo.

Late that night I marvelled at the peaceful sight of my dark-haired children tucked alongside the blond heads of our host children. Kelowna had literally moved over in bed, making room for 30,000 neighbours to crawl in.

Our family grew from five to eight as we picked up our teenage children, home from summer jobs. Our host mom would laugh and say "the more the merrier," as she peeled more potatoes.

On coming home, our neighbourhood was unscathed. Each night we would go out on the street to chat, watching together as the fire crept closer again, wondering how long we could stay.

The trauma was nearly over for us, but the lessons were not. Though it was promised, my husband's regular job was not held for him while he worked the fire. It felt like a kick in the teeth. Temporarily out of work with three daughters leaving for college and our own suitcases packed by the door left me depressed. It got the better of me as tears and anger gushed out at the fire. I asked God, "What more could go wrong?" Stupid question, considering. That night I walked the street alone.

At the fence with the best view, I looked up to the nearby ridge. The fire stood balanced on the pinnacle, reaching its terrible tendrils hundreds, maybe thousands of feet into the night sky. People said they could see it from Armstrong. It looked like the hand of God held it there, keeping all hell from sweeping down the hillside towards the houses and orchards. I never imagined seeing the hand of God this side of heaven, but there it was, clearly displayed in all its grandeur, big as the fire but much stronger. My soul relented and I knew that a lot more could go wrong should that hand let go. I understood better what we were spared from and realized how much God protects me from things I can't see.

OKANAGAN FIRESTORM
BY DONA MCINTYRE

Blood-red, purple, green gone.

Deer foraging for food in the backyards of houses no longer standing.

Grass tasting to these small creatures, like the nectar of the gods.

God help us.

Black, crisp, chunks of trees surrounded by sullen smoke, twirling around the stumps.

Dark smoldering ashes.

Heat choking,

so hot it's hard to breathe.

So hard to see death everywhere.

Green dying.

Soft round animal eyes crying out of the blackness, that was once so cool and full of tiny soft shoots of new life,

now stomped down into the dusty peppery earth

by the filthy dirty boot of the firestorm

quickly killing everything

in its path,

from the largest with keen intelligence, full of fear, to the smallest, most innocent creatures.

Then hungrily attacking us, consuming our hopes and dreams for the future,

consuming even our pasts, as it ravages our homes and treasured memories.

We beg for help.

There is none.

We watch, helpless, as nature throws her weight around like a drunken bully, insulted and raging in a barroom brawl, knowing

we have little control other than the way we deal with loss.

Loss of forest green, and creatures great and small.

Loss of houses, boats, cars.

All burned as if some great and powerful hand put pen to earth and circled those to be omitted, hurriedly deciding what will sta☐☐

and what will go,

and yet, not one human life is lost,

not one innocent,

not one defiant,

not one who fought to save us.

Like some powerful hand put pen to earth and circled those to be omitted.

Yes, circled all.

Angels at Seton House
by Madeleine Allen

On August 19, 2003, St. Elizabeth Ann Seton House of Prayer was put on evacuation alert. Two women on retreat were praying in the chapel on the hill and had a sense of angels surrounding Seton House. Another person praying had the sense of Seton House surrounded by fire but not burned.

On August 21, Gene Allen, the caretaker of Seton House, was standing outside watching the fire on the hill with his son Kevin. He saw a red ball a little below the fire in the trees and said to Kevin, "Is that fire?" With that, the whole tree exploded into flame, then the one next to it. Within minutes, the whole side of the hill was on fire.

They decided they better leave when a fireman came up and gave them evacuation orders. Kevin asked how much time they had. He said twenty minutes to half an hour, then turned his head and his eyes became as large as saucers. "Get into your vehicles, let's get out of here!"

As they raced down the hill, the fire was already at the fire break at the side of the road. Sometimes when the road twisted, it looked like they were driving right into the fire. It was a harrowing experience.

Days passed watching the fire, not knowing if anything could possibly be left. Rumours abounded. A week or so later, tour buses were arranged to take homeowners into the burned out area to see their property. Gene and Father Don Wilson, the chaplain and administrator of Seton House, tried to get on the bus going into the Chute Lake Road area. They were denied as the bus wasn't going that far.

Days of frustration followed trying to get up to see what happened to Seton House and Father Don's house next door. One day they would hear that everything was fine, the next they'd hear both had burned. Finally, a staff sergeant was able to make arrangements for Gene to get past the check points.

The power poles to Seton House had burned so there was no electricity. Father Don's house was burnt to the ground. The twelve-foot cedars lining the drive were burnt up to the car port. The fascia board of the carport was singed, but the carport was otherwise untouched.

For several days, Gene was able to get up to Seton House to keep an eye on things. The army suppression crew used Seton's parking lot as their staging area.

After five days, Gene was evacuated again and not allowed up. Getting past the check points proved difficult for the next month. Anyone coming to Seton House had to register until the end of September. Firemen were called to put out hotspots until November.

Gene's favourite spot to take visitors to Seton House is to show them a tree. There are deep holes around it where other trees and their roots were burnt but this large tree, approximately eighteen inches in diameter, was burnt black up to a round smooth spot where a branch had been removed and a ceramic cross put on the spot. The black burn circles the cross and its little smooth spot and then continues for another four feet. The cross was not melted but plastic irrigation pipes in the ground where the trees were not burned melted.

We stand here amazed and thank God for saving Seton House. We are an oasis of green circled by a burnt out forest. The fire came to a few feet from the chapel on the hill to the south and to the north up to a few inches from the main building. On the east, across the road, Father Don's residence was burnt. On the west side, the fire burned up to approximately twenty-five feet behind the caretaker's home.

New life rises from ashes and we are grateful.

Chapter
Eight
Through a Child's Eye

"It made me feel sad that peoples houses burned down. I wish we wouldn't have any more fires."

REUBEN WEST SOAMES, AGE 8

"The fire was very smoky, we had to hold our breath to go outside. I wanted to go up and stop the fire by myself. I worried about the firefighters. They were very brave."

KIRSTEN TANNER, AGE 8

MY HORROR STORY
BY TWYLA SPITTLE <small>GRADE 5</small>

This fire experience felt like the end of the world! I could hear fire truck sirens every second. The sky was the colour of blood.

When I looked out my bedroom window the night I got evacuated, I saw monstrous red flames! My family and I went outside and saw a firetruck across the street! The firefighters were spraying our neighbour's houses! Scared and frightened I quickly ran back inside. I was in my room for a little while until... the doorbell rang! I ran downstairs and there standing in my doorway was a female firefighter! She told us in a calm, stern voice that we had to evacuate in one hour!!! The firefighter left in a hurry! Crying and weeping I dragged myself to pack up my stuffies and valuable items. My mom packed up frightened and worried, my dad's face was pale. In one hour we left the house and that was the last time I ever saw it again.

FIRE, FIRE BY SIMON CHARLES EDWARDS GRADE 6

FIRE, FIRE,
BURNING
BRIGHT,
LIKE A CANDLE
IN
THE NIGHT
FIREFIGHTERS
TRIED IN
VAIN
BUT THAT
FIRE IS SUCH A
PAIN!

Okanagan Mountain Park Fire

by Shelby Holler, grade 5

Weeoo, weeoo! The police car came roaring down my street!!! I knew that meant we had to leave. My head was stuffed with mind twisting thoughts about the fire. I breathed in the air that smelled like thick burning ash. I looked up at the sky at the billowing red smoke circling my home. That was the last thing before I left.

At the hotel I sat looking out the window at the monstrous flames leaping out from behind the tall black mountains. I felt like I was dead only I was sitting there alive. My heart was beating so loudly in my chest that it felt like a drum. The fire affected lots of people and some were even left homeless but this fire did bring our community together in many different ways, and that is an important thing.

The Community Pulled Together

by Kylie Wilson, grade 5

The Okanagan Mountain Fire was surprising to my family and me. We had such a great summer. Then, all of a sudden, gigantic orange and yellow flames came roaring down the mountain towards our home.

Evacuation was the most terrifying part for me. I had been playing with my friend, who had just gone home. The house was quieter than usual, I was watching the tremendous flames out the window and mom and dad were in the kitchen making dinner. All of a sudden I heard my mom say in a worried voice, "Oh, no, they're coming!"

Before I could ask my mom what she meant, a loud, eardrum-breaking siren went off outside. Peering out the window, I saw a police car inching its way down our street. A tall thin man in it was bellowing into a microphone, "YOU MUST EVACUATE YOUR HOME IMMEDIATELY!" I sprang into action letting out a whimper of terror. Scrambling all around the house, I collected all my belongings. Although it was a very sad and scary time, the community pulled together to help one another.

THE FIRE
BY LUCY PRESCOTT GRADE 6

The lightning strikes,
A fire is started,
A few days later,
Late at night,
Cars line up down the street.
Through the window
I see the fire climbing
down the hills,
Pushed by the wind.
The next day we are evacuated.
We stay up on a hill with friends,
Away from the fire.
We looked through
their telescope,
And saw houses burning
to the ground.
Smoke is everywhere.
There is ash and burned
stuff on the ground.
We are now safe back
in our homes.
Others are less
Fortunate than us,
And no longer have homes.
But we have already started
to rebuild our community.

The Forest Fire

by Katherine Kitura, grade 5

The Okanagan Mountain Park Fire was life changing for all of us. People stood on their balconies with binoculars watching the smoke curving and twisting up like a snake. When I went outside to watch the fire I could immediately smell the heavy smoke hanging like a cloud above us. It smelled so bad I could hardly breathe. The sky was dark red and the sun looked like a giant ball of flames. It looked so scary!

"Reeoo, Reeooo!" We heard the sirens coming closer to our house. Next thing you know we were evacuated. At night from the Westside, we could clearly see the red hot flames sweeping through the mountains. The flames looked so terrifying that I wept in fear. We went outside and we saw huge flames towering over the trees. My mom said the houses were on fire. We always listened to the radio to find out if we could go home. They said 30,000 people were evacuated! When we finally got home I was so happy and grateful! I hope our community never has to go through that again!

THE DRAGON
BY JIM PLOVER GRADE 6

The fire was blazing
The smoke smelled,
The heat was intense,
it burned,
it destroyed homes.

The firefighters are
achieving a goal!
But the fire torched trees.
The loud noise
the ash got thrown
everywhere.
The firefighters
can hardly contain
the dragon!

There was hope
and
sadness.
The people looked helpless,
They could do nothing.

MONSTER IN THE MOUNTAINS
BY JEN JASCHKE GRADE 6

There is a Monster in the Mountains

raging higher and higher

as the wind whips by.

The evil,

horrific monster

rushes down the mountain,

There were homes destroyed

by evil flames

People rushing out of their homes to safety

Animal

habitat destroyed

by raging flames

animals die,

hopefully the evil monster will too.

FIERY BLAZE
BY DJ STREILEIN AGE 14

White clouds turn to gray,
Darker and darker by the day,
Green hills turn ablaze,
City streets start to haze,
Mother Nature starts to rage,
Placing us in a fiery cage,
Scorching the mountain side,
Our firefighters will not abide,
The fire snake moving fast,
Torching everything that it has passed,
Lighting up the hills with fiery embers,
Threatening the city and all its members,
Fire fighters from east to west,
Come from all around and do their best,
Fire fighters from north to south,
Heading straight into its fiery mouth,
It burns never seeming to need a rest,
Putting our skills to the ultimate test,
To fight this dangerous fire snake,
Worst case scenario we do not fake,
As it continues to burn at a rapid pace,
Almost as if it were a race,
As it moves across our hills,
Filling our lives with dangerous thrills,
Seeing the huge fire,
Everyone's safety is the only desire,
We pray to all the good graces,
That we will be able to put smiles on everyone's faces,
Our support goes out to all,
Until this fire will finally fall,
We must work together in this fight
And set all this wrong back to right.

FIRES
BY ASHLEE MCEACHERN GRADE 8

I hear the sound of fire trucks,

Not able to see what's going on,

I see the flames rising higher and higher,

The blue sky getting darker,

As the smoke starts to rise,

Next you hear a knock on the door,

Feared to answer it,

As the door opens,

You hear a voice,

"Take a few things and leave your house."

Nothing to say,

As you leave your house,

Asking yourself,

Will you ever see it again?

Fire in Okanagan Mountain
by Amanda Krehel, grade 5

I felt a sudden rage as the fire crept towards my home and my neighbourhood went on evacuation alert. People stood on their driveways watching the flames come down the hill towards their homes. The next night winds swirled in all directions and smoke filled the air.

About one hour later the sirens went off and we were evacuated. When we got settled in at the Best Western my neighbour and I went to the top of the tower. We watched the tall billowing clouds of smoke and fire move quickly across the hill. When I saw the raging flames through my hotel window that night it felt like the whole city was going to burn and that I would have nowhere to go. I remember the excitement of my family when they found out we could go back to our home. When I got back I felt as if the fire had damaged me more than it damaged my neighbours' homes. Then I stood in my bedroom doorway thinking that I was very fortunate to have a home.

THE MONSTER OF THE MOUNTAINS
BY ALYSSA SHAY GRADE 6

Hazy and smoky all around
Cars coming up and down the road
Lots of helicopters dropping water
On the Monster in the Mountains.

People rushing, yet trying to stay calm
Firefighters and police knocking on doors
Stuck in a traffic jam, keeping a lookout
On the Monster in the Mountains.

Hot and tired, tension in the air
Wonder and panic have taken over
Firefighters' courage is a challenge
For the Monster in the Mountains.

22 000 hectares long
many homes lost, despair at its worst
misery, impatience, horror and billowing all
for the Monster in the Mountains.

GHOST MOUNTAINS
BY VANESSA VOLPATTI AGE 15

The early dawn is breaking,
But you cannot see the sun rise,
Thick grey smoke consumes you,
Burning in your eyes.
Some are rushed from their houses,
With little time to pack,
Some only got out,
With what they had on their backs.
This monster so frightful,
And so hard to fight,
But they never stop to rest or sleep
Until the morning light.
It comes in waves,
And leaves destruction in its wake,
Anything it can touch,
It reaches out and takes.
Air is its fuel,
And the forest and homes are a feast,
But nothing will cure the hunger,
Of this atrocious beast.

We commend the people,
Who fight just as hard,
But with everything they do,
They need to be dealt the right cards.
We need to thank people,
That aren't really thought about
Even the simple deeds,
Can really help out.
And as we gaze through our windows,
At a world left behind,
Smoke still fills the air,
But a thought stays in your mind.
These ghost mountains will leave,
And the sky will clear,
Things will grow back,
But it will take years.
So we will be strong,
And rebuild together,
We are a community, a family,
Now and forever.

Chapter Nine
Animal Tales

"We return to Joe Rich to try to evacuate our old horse, Spotty, but she is not a good trailer rider. Eventually, she loads, with the help of a neighbour, but kicks and lurches all the way down. She seems to have sweated off about 50 pounds!"

REG VOLK

"Grim-faced, we unload the horses and lead them to the pasture. 'If it gets too close, we'll run 'em to the river,' says Fergie. The matter-of-fact-ness of his statement diminishes my fear. I understand from his confidence that it wouldn't be the first time he's had to save horses from fire."

ROSS TYNER

HOW LISA NEARLY GOT ARRESTED

BY KATE ALEXANDER

Last summer our busy household consisted of my partner Lisa and me, our houseguests Michael and Sarah from Vancouver, and our beloved dog (or is that god?) Quinn. Sarah was acting in 'A Midsummer Night's Dream' at the Mission Hill Winery.

The fire had started on a ridge visible from our dock and initially seemed to be moving uphill and away from us. Lisa and Michael spent much time exclaiming whenever a tree candled, while singing every fire song they remembered. On the other side of the lake, Sarah's audience was distracted: the outdoor theatre also offered an excellent view of the fire.

Thursday night, August 22, we had been on a one-hour evacuation alert for three days. With no wind, the town had been enveloped in thick yellowish smoke, looking like smog but smelling oddly like a campfire. This lack of view gave us a sense of security. After work we had dinner in a restaurant downtown, and then walked over to the theatre to see the musical *Cabaret*. We were entranced by the show: good music, wonderful dancing and acting. At the end I was emotionally overcome (embarrassing when you're in the front row, but apparently actors like to see their audience in tears).

As we left the theatre, Michael, looking very distraught, found us. "Get home right now, the fire has come down over the mountain. You need to get Quinn!"

Lisa drove. I wouldn't have been capable. We reached the roadblock where Michael and Sarah had been turned back, having only Vancouver identification. We could now see flames on the hillside. Up the road to the Chute Lake junction and at the second flashing yellow light was another roadblock, staffed by volunteers – the auxiliary RCMP. They were under orders not to let anyone through despite our pleading that we lived only five hundred metres further on. Thoughts of Quinn panicked in a burning house made my stomach turn. But Lisa has guts. She started driving, slowly and deliberately, towards our home. Part way there, an oncoming police car did a U turn, came up behind us with lights flashing and then tried to overtake us when Lisa didn't pull over. But the cop passed us just as Lisa swung into our driveway on the right. Three police cars with lights and sirens followed us down the long driveway in a sort of O.J. Simpson slow chase. At the bottom, Lisa swerved the truck so I'd have cover as I darted to the front door. I guess she thought they'd have weapons aimed at us, hardened criminals that we are.

Quinn was terrified. He'd have heard volunteers knocking at the door all evening. Never was he so glad to jump in the truck. Lisa, meanwhile, had the cops threatening to put her in handcuffs and tow her truck back to the station. Then, we became aware of our landlord's dog Jake barking, so I decided to rescue him. But Bill, our landlord and next-door neighbour, appeared, too. That provided enough of a distraction for me to go back into the house and for the cops to think twice about arresting Lisa while they had Bill sign a waiver allowing him to stay in his house. As I looked around for essentials we had forgotten (Lisa didn't tell me her clothing bag with passport and insurance documents were still upstairs), the phone rang. It was Sarah - what amazing timing! "Get my cosmetic bag - I need my glasses!" That, and a bucket of dog food, that precious commodity, was all I got before a police officer hauled me out of the house.

By one o'clock in the morning, we had found sanctuary at a friend's house in Westbank. Michael and Sarah had a place to stay downtown with some acting friends. We later found out that the evacuation order, involving ten percent of the town's population, had come in at 6:00 p.m. Why no one in the theatre or restaurant had announced it remains a mystery.

The next evening, like most Okanagan Mission residents, we watched the fire wreak its worst havoc safely from the Westside. We brought our telescope to a place with a sweeping view of Kelowna and Okanagan Mountain Park. The subdivisions just south of our house were a vision of hell – we could see house frames and chimneys silhouetted by flames. Further north the fire had moved inland and was shooting from treetop to treetop. Using the pyramid of Summerhill Winery as a landmark, we were able to locate our house. Not burning. In fact we could see lights left on at Bill's. But up the two gullies on either side there were houses on fire. Subdued, we went to bed, not knowing whether we'd have a home in the morning.

We viewed the devastation of the night before in Saturday's bright sunlight. Our house stood. And though we could see places that had burned, devastation wasn't by any means total. Even in the "vision of hell" neighbourhood, houses had survived. But for many, that was no comfort. Two hundred and thirty-eight houses had burned down, seemingly at random. Soon, the television showed these neighbourhoods: typically, we'd see a nice green lawn, bright flowerbeds, a swimming pool with a few cinders in it, and nothing but a pit in the ground where a house had been.

There hasn't been a court summons for Lisa. I regret that we caused extra work for already stressed police officers and volunteers who had a huge, frightening, and unfamiliar workload. But I have absolutely no regret that we broke the law to save our dog. Lisa's fighting spirit and ability to think and act in a crisis have deepened my love and admiration for her.

Rocket and the Canucks

by Jerry Rawson

By 6:30 p.m. on August 21 I had been at the animal in-take section of Emergency Social Services for almost eight hours. A rumour was spreading that we were going to shut down for the night because everything seemed so quiet. It couldn't have been 15 minutes later that half of our group gathered a few essentials and drove off to the new Kelowna Secondary School to set up a second reception centre. Ten thousand people were being evacuated!

Even for those who remained at Parkinson Rec. Centre, the evening became very busy very quickly. Sometime after 10 p.m., a man in his mid-twenties with a pit bull on a choke chain and sturdy lead, attracted the attention of everyone at our end of the large room. The dog seemed interested in eating anything that had more than two legs, excluding possibly tables and chairs. People who could pick up their pets did so; others subtly established defensive positions and obscured their pet's view of the dreaded dog.

A volunteer asked the man to take his dog to the back of the building so we could deal with it without so many distractions. Outside we discovered that Emergency Social Services had assigned the man a hotel room, but the hotel would not accept his dog.

Another volunteer phoned Glenmora Kennels and they unhesitatingly agreed to take the pit bull. However, the man couldn't get his dog there.

Despite the fact that I don't really trust pit bulls, I was allowed to volunteer. When I asked the man how to get his dog in the truck, he replied, "Just open the door and say, 'Rocket, car ride!'" So I delivered my line and watched Rocket shoot onto the driver's seat, bounce once, then alertly take his position on the passenger seat, peering out the front window, only too eager to get going. I slipped in, sorted out the lead for Rocket's choke chain and we were off.

We didn't become best friends, but our ride was uneventful. Rocket stayed on his side, glaring intently into the outer darkness, apparently edgily content. I was happy, as long as he was. At the kennels I kept a tight rein as Rocket eagerly scanned the menu, but we opened a kennel and locked him in before he could sample anything. And that was that.

As I returned to the Rec Centre I got my first glimpse that night of the extent to which the destruction on the mountains had grown. Inside I joined the volunteers who were taking information from people looking for temporary homes for their pets. I picked up a pen and watched a young couple's hesitant approach. The woman was cradling a blue-lidded Tupperware bowl. I invited them to sit as she cautiously admitted that they needed a foster home for a half-dozen goldfish!

I worked my way through the in-take form: Does your pet have a tag? A tattoo? Does your pet have a collar? A leash? Are your pet's vaccinations up-to-date? Does your pet have a tail? Is it long? Short? Are its ears floppy? Erect? What is your pet's name?

"They each have a name," she confessed, "but as a group we call them the Canucks." I put the whole team on one form and labelled their blue lid accordingly. I heard later that Wal-Mart partitioned an aquarium, the Canucks did the duration in the pet department and even Bertuzzi behaved!

Kitty's Tale

by Adele and Doug Glennie

Our Okanagan Mountain Park Fire experience is mild compared to those who fought the fires, volunteered for hours on end, were evacuated, or lost their homes, but I feel compelled to tell the story just the same.

On the Saturday morning after the big fire, we decided to go down to the evacuation centres to see if we could lend a hand. Our first stop was the Parkinson Recreation Centre, but we had just missed the volunteer orientation session, so we decided to go to Kelowna Secondary School instead. Once there, we found there was another overwhelming response from volunteers and as we waited, we stopped at the SPCA table and learned of the need for foster homes for displaced animals. The SPCA was our next stop.

The SPCA staff was busy cleaning the building, organizing volunteers and waiting for animals to arrive. We learned that they had evacuated all their animals to other locations because of the alert they were under. We told the staff we would gladly take a cat or two, filled out the information sheet and proceeded to wait. While waiting, we heard the story of Hitman, the Llama. Hitman was reportedly seen in several yards in East Kelowna but every time the SPCA got a call to rescue him, he moved off to another location. We quickly decided that if Hitman were rescued, our yard would not accommodate him and we would stick to the tameness of a domesticated feline. Boy, were we wrong about that!

After a while, a volunteer brought in a beautiful, fluffy, calico cat that was found on Drummond Court on the back porch of an evacuated home. She was smelly, dirty and frightened but appeared to be unscathed by the fire. We instantly fell in love with her, started calling her "Kitty" (what else?) and gently put her in the SPCA's cardboard carrying case to take her home. This would be our small contribution to helping our community.

Kitty travelled well, only piddling in her box and down my leg once. No major harm done there! Once home, we decided it would be best to keep her separate from the rest of the house in our spare room in the basement so she could acclimatize to her new surroundings. We thought it would also be good for our own cats to be introduced slowly to the new arrival. So Kitty lived in the lap of luxury, with her own leather chair to sit in, a TV for her amusement and a treadmill, should she decide she needed some exercise! We visited with her often and she quickly decided she liked to curl up in our laps, lick our hands and sleep contentedly on her leather chair.

After a couple of hours, we thought it time for Kitty to meet the 'owners' of the house, our cats Puck and Blu. We let her out of her room and she tentatively explored the basement and ventured out into the foyer. Our cats knew something was up, but they graciously kept their distance until Kitty decided to get closer. We thought they were being very welcoming hosts until we heard the most horrible hissing and growling sounds. As it turned out, Kitty was not a very pleasant houseguest! Every time our cats came anywhere near her, her claws came out, her tail got all fluffy, she arched her back, and bared her teeth. How rude! Nevertheless, we gave Kitty the benefit of the doubt, knowing she was probably traumatized by the whole experience.

In the meantime, Puck, our big, 25 pound male cat, ran and hid under the nearest piece of furniture every time Kitty came anywhere near him. Even Blu, the more gregarious of the two, decided she was no match for Kitty and kept her distance. We thought that with some time, Kitty would decide that they were no threat to her and would eventually come around. No such luck though. Kitty dominated the house and we eventually had to sequester her to her room again.

We took turns visiting her and she was as friendly as could be to us. Our daughter spent hours with her, watching videos in Kitty's room. She was just lovely to the new humans in her life. After a couple of days, we decided to try again but Kitty would have nothing to do with her feline counterparts. She chased our cats out of the basement and proceeded to play with all their toys, eat their food and cosy up to their humans. We could tell they were not pleased with the situation and our commitment to our evacuee remained steady, although we were secretly hoping that Kitty had an owner who would want her back and was not a stray, because then what would we do?

After five days of fostering Kitty, we learned that Drummond Road area residents had returned home. We hadn't heard from the SPCA that they had located her owner, so we took it upon ourselves to drive there and see if we could locate them. We had become attached to Kitty in a short time, even though she was quite bossy to our other "children." Her parting shot as she left the house was to hiss menacingly at Puck as he made a beeline for under the couch.

We knew the address where Kitty was found so my husband went up and knocked on the door. Kitty had become very excited in the truck so we knew she was aware that she was near her home. A very surprised and happy mother and her nine year old son came down the driveway and took Kitty into their arms. Their gratitude needed no words as we saw the look of relief and love on their faces. Petra, Kitty's owner, told us that her real name was Mitzi and that she lived with a big German Shepherd. This would account for her need to be assertive! In any event, Mitzi and her owners were reunited and we felt happy to do our small part for our community in their time of need. We still look at pictures we took of Mitzi while she was in our care, and agree that we would do it all over again.

The Little Red Squirrel

by Nicole Conduit-Hunter

There was this little red squirrel that used to drive my dad crazy. It lived in a big tree just outside the kitchen. It had a food supply nearby in the form of a birdfeeder and a little pond to drink from. What more could it want? Every time my mom or dad went to fill the birdfeeder this little squirrel would chatter away very noisily at them. It used to get very angry when either of my parents went outside and especially when their dog was around. This little squirrel would just sit on the lowest branch and chatter on and on because my parents were obviously interfering with its collection of food.

Everyday dad grumbled about how this little thing kept taking all the birdseed and leaving nothing for the birds. During some of my visits I would catch my dad running out the door and yelling at the squirrel. He was even seen picking up a few pinecones and throwing them in the general direction of the squirrel in a vain attempt to deter it from coming back. The fact that the pinecones never made it within 5 feet of the squirrel was a source of amusement for both my mom and me.

I got a call from my dad the day after the lightning strike. From then on the updates came day by day then hour by hour until I couldn't stand it anymore. I got on a plane and went out to help my parents. By the time I got there the only help left to give was emotional. The fate of their home was up to the winds. My parents' home is in the Lakeshore & Timberline area. I got there the day of the firestorm.

It wasn't until 13 days later that we were allowed back to the house. We did have a house to go to but my parents lived on a beautiful property surrounded by trees. As we drove up we could see the devastation that had occurred. Some of the hottest spots of the fire had been on my parents' property. As we got closer to the house we could see only a few green trees. It was almost like a little green oasis around the house. Basically whatever the sprinklers had touched and soaked remained green. We walked around inside and out in disbelief, looking at the inches between where a cinder had obviously landed and a wooden deck. Everything was so quiet. There wasn't the sound of birds or even the wind in the trees.

Then as we were all standing in the kitchen we heard it. The unmistakable sound of that little red squirrel. It was sitting on its branch and chattering on. We all had tears in our eyes and my dad couldn't move fast enough to get some birdseed to take out to it. He dumped a big bowl of seed on the ground and in the feeder and was so grateful for the squirrel's survival.

It's January now and the squirrel is still around and my dad is still happily feeding it.

Dining with Ducks

by Ken Levert, Chief Petty Officer, retired

I was with the Navy Team that deployed from CFB Esquimalt on Sept. 03. We were Navy Wave 1 (affectionately known as "Tsunami") and were 100 strong. We travelled to Camp Vernon to be issued firefighting kits and receive an updated situation report on the fire. The next day we arrived in Camp Kelowna and proceeded to erect tents and prepare for operations.

Our mornings begin at 05:30. Get up, hit the washroom trailers, assemble kit, go for breakfast, grab a lunch and head out for the trucks that brought us up the mountain. It was a new scenario for almost every sailor, soldier, and airman in our force, but our structured leadership and experienced senior non-commissioned members made everything fall into place and work.

Driving through the streets of Kelowna in our army trucks, wearing our red, yellow and orange firefighting coveralls, made us a magnet for the citizens to wave at or honk at. It was a great feeling. And the signs erected at many business sites, as well as at many private residences, were very heart warming. It felt great to be assisting our own countrymen in their time of need.

There were more than 700 military personnel in Camp Kelowna at the Apple Bowl. Those included Army regiments, an Air Force contingent, and Navy. It was at the Navy supply tent that two wild ducks dined for breakfast and supper. The other units were justifiably jealous but Peking and L'Orange (as we nicknamed them) were loyal to us and loved Navy rations.

I can't applaud loudly enough for the support we received in camp. There were ample washroom facilities, porta-potties, laundry facilities, TVs in our mess tent, and some of the best food I've ever eaten in military establishments anywhere, provided by the cooks in the portable kitchens.

A group of us returned later for the city's celebration at the end of the fires. The parade route lined with citizens and the ceremony in the arena brought a lump to my throat.

I am now retired from the Navy but will always remember my experience in Kelowna.

ONE FARM GONE
BY JOAN CURRIE

On the night the awesome lightning struck,
Hurtling, climbing flames careened amuck;
Who knew its fury? winds helped create,
A forest that burned at a magnificent rate.

Homes in its path, thousands had to leave,
Belongings? barely time to retrieve;
Pets fearful, hiding, some left behind,
Some rescued, others no one could find.

Doors and windows had to be kept closed,
Somehow the smoke still seeped inside;
The news: Thousands more evacuated,
Off and on I felt so bad I cried!

As the days went on and still no sign,
That the fire would die, no more ORANGE sunshine;
For the Mountain Park Fire still fiercely raged,
While firefighters/soldiers the good fight waged.

Friends of ours... a family of four,
Moved one horse Westside, still had three more;
Next day tri-trailered steeds to other ground,
Unknowing the flames were that way bound.

These poor fillies were 'trucked' again next day
To the safer field offered they'd stay;
That night our friends ordered, LEAVE RIGHT AWAY –
And in the fire's path their farm now lay.

Stashed quickly in bags some of their clothes,
Whatever they most needed... who knows?
Carried out dogs, cats, made the get-away fast;
To their church where they'd be safe at last.

We relied on T.V. for all we could learn,
Then came the rumour our friend's farm had burned;
I couldn't digest that news in my head,
So, waited a day to phone them instead.

T'was the husband who answered the phone,
Instinctively knew the caller was 'Joan'
I asked whether the rumours were true,
The answer, though, I unconsciously knew!

As he related the details... of how
Their house, their barn, and shed were all burned,
None were allowed to return, see their place;
Listening, huge tears rolled down my face!

I was filled with extreme emotion,
As he ventured these wise words to say;
Comprehending his deep devotion,
Hearing where his thoughts and cares most lay.

He said,

"We're rich, not to have suffered loss of life,
For I've my two daughters and dear wife;
There's our dogs and cats... we have each horse,
God has provided, we've no remorse.
Buildings are only made out of wood –
But we all have hope and that is good."

Out of the ashes people will rebuild,
New grass will grow where the land is tilled –
When the fire's out, they'll plant new trees,
We'll see blue skies, feel the gentle breeze;

There's so much to thank God for,
And our stories and poems will become folklore!

The Incredible Journey
by Angela Schouten

I've always loved my cousin's big black fluffy kitty cat, Norton. I had even gotten one exactly like it myself, only to find I was allergic to the beautiful long angora-like cat fur.

The night of the big evacuation, Thursday, August 21, my cousin Rhonda called me from the coast and asked me to jump in my car at 11:00 p.m. and go rescue her two birds, her cat, and jewellery from her Crawford Estate home. I grabbed a fistful of garbage bags and took off with my neighbour John. It was quite an awe inspiring sight as we saw a huge wall of flame behind her house and a steady line of traffic making a mass exodus down the mountain. We knew we were experiencing a once in a lifetime (we hope) event along with the rest of our fellow Kelownians, and it was a terrifying experience to see such urgency on all the faces we passed in the cars.

We arrived at her house and I phoned her in Vancouver and said, "It's a sheer wall of flame back here; I can't imagine how your house is going to make it through this!"

John and I proceeded to toss clothing, purses, jewellery, heirlooms, and pictures – everything my little Tracker could hold – into garbage bags. Then we loaded the birds in their cages, and finally, precious big old Norton, in a makeshift box with a sled taped on the top of it. I raced the animals down the mountain to my home near High Road and spent the next while making them comfortable in my garage/break-dance studio.

Each day for the next four days, I lovingly tended to the animals. Norton seemed to really like it at my house, so I began giving him a little extra space to roam. That was my biggest mistake because just when I thought I could trust my wonderful black fluffy friend, he decided to take off on me. I was horrified, as anyone who has "pet-sat" can well imagine, to find Norton had disappeared. I called and called for him, I visited neighbours, I went up to complete strangers and demanded to know if their cats (who looked black and fluffy) were really my beloved Norton... to no avail. My cousin's husband was especially attached to the animal and got a trap from the SPCA made for trapping cats and set it up in my yard. Well, that silly trap began trapping neighbours' cats! And man alive, did that ever make me a whole lot of enemies... I had neighbours threatening to sue me and calling me all sorts of names.

Well, Norton the runaway cat seemed irrevocably gone, so, in a last ditch effort, I pounded the pavement of my neighbourhood once again, this time putting up signs on all the lamp posts, growing more desperate by the minute, as I realized that I would be seeing my cousin and her family every birthday and holiday in between, and did not want this on my conscience, let alone how awful I felt to think the cat was wandering somewhere.

Well, will wonders ever cease! Here's where all of a sudden heaven parted and a ray of sunshine spilled forth, for 17 days later, my cousin called me first thing in the morning and said, "You'll never guess who showed up on my doorstep this morning!"... I couldn't dare to hope... then she continued, "It's Norton!"

Norton must have walked all the way home! That's a long 15 kilometres, across Highway 97, over Springfield Road, K.L.O. Road, and many other busy streets, bridges, up mountains - we just couldn't believe it! Rhonda continued, "He looks terribly thin and scraggly but he's here and we are just rejoicing!"

Her three boys were so elated they couldn't stop hugging him. Rhonda promptly gave him two big bowls of tuna and let him recline in the sunshine on the down comforter in her bedroom for a few days. The cat came back!! 17 days later!! Through hill and dale, that cat was so determined he walked for 15 kilometres. We treat him with a lot more reverence now that we see his fortitude and dedication to the family. He is one wonderful feline!

I Just Want to Go Home
by Janice Casling

On August 16, 2003, we heard the lightning strike on the hill above Squally Point, smelled the smoke. That night, my friend Gord phoned; he'd been put on evacuation alert and told to get his horses out. We hooked up our trailer and headed out. It looked like we were driving towards Armageddon. Little did we know, it was just the beginning.

We drove past the road blocks, loading the horses in the dark and smoke. One of them was so frightened she wouldn't be caught. We took extra time and coaxed her to hop in loose with her friends. I hoped we wouldn't have to move them again.

Tuesday Gord's neighbourhood was evacuated. Wednesday I convinced my hubby we had to get our animals out. I didn't want to be rushing to move them in a last minute panic.

By the time I contacted my friend in Lumby, it was dark. I loaded my horse Bentley, who went in willingly, but then panicked and backed out fast, hitting his tail and hip on the door. I didn't know if he was okay or not but coaxed him back in and the sheep behind him.

We left them in a dark field in Lumby. I hoped Bentley was going to be fine – he's part horse, part human and my buddy. I hated to leave him like that. When we drove back into Kelowna near midnight, ash was falling like snow in the headlights. I knew we had made the right decision.

Thursday I called Gord. We had to move his horses from our fields. We hauled them to a farm near OUC's North Campus. On our way out, fire trucks met us with sirens blaring, heading up to our area. The radio said there was a fire in Myra Canyon. I felt an icy grip on my stomach, my dog was at home alone. We unloaded the horses and raced back. The fire was contained, but I was rattled. I vowed not to leave again without my dog. I had been avoiding packing anything, not wanting to admit it was coming, but now I knew it was. I could now take a photo of our house and the fire in the same frame.

Uneasy but tired, we went to bed. The phone rang almost immediately. We had volunteered our trailer and it was a warning we would be needed soon. We just hung up and it rang again – the next door neighbour needed horses moved. As we got dressed, we saw the convoy of trucks and trailers rushing down June Springs Road. Almost immediately, there were fire trucks all through the neighbourhood with sirens blaring. My heart started racing as I accomplished the packing I couldn't bring myself to do earlier. The dog inside the crate in the car, cat in another and kitty litter, I grabbed clothes, pictures, emptied the meat from the deepfreeze and Mike parked the tractor, small truck and lawnmower in the middle of the greenest field.

That night, Gord's neighbourhood burned. Friday we were allowed home for one hour but after standing in line to get our permit, only had 20 minutes of that hour left. We hauled out what we could but forgot socks and underwear, the binoculars and cell phone charger – all things we later needed. I took one last look around and said goodbye to my house.

As we sat mesmerized in front of the TV, watching flames spread across the hillside, we recognized the three lights above our farm and saw the flames were nearly there. We woke a few hours later, sure our farm was gone. I cried for my barn cat I'd left behind. I looked at what I had saved and wondered what I hadn't. We went for a drive and as we crested the hill on Dilworth, I could see our area was not burned.

The most frustrating and frightening feeling for me was that I could not go home. My dog, a neurotic border collie, could not live this life of driving around or living in a crate, so I took her to Lumby where I had dropped off the horse and sheep the week before.

We tried applying for an agricultural pass to pick our blueberry crop, but because of a line on a map, were not issued one. They told us the house had been gelled and no one was getting in.

The next day we were allowed home. I went to Lumby and got my dog, who seemed a little disappointed to be leaving the sheep behind. We drove to the farm and it looked better than we had left it. The rain that night of the firestorm washed the layer of ash into the soil.

After assurances the fire was all but controlled, we went to Lumby September 1st and picked up the sheep and my horse. We even brought extra sheep to graze in exchange for ours being cared for there, but the next evening, we watched water bombers overhead along with the helicopters. The peaceful evening was shattered by a convoy of fire trucks racing down the hill. They told us to leave right away.

I had no where to take 31 sheep, and what about my horse? I loaded him up, got back to the house to pack things once again, and put the cat and dog back in the car. I left a frantic message for my friend in Lumby, the sheep would have to stay; the field was green, there was lots of water and hopefully they'd survive.

This time it seemed serious. I could see flames in the sky above our farm. Once the animals were loaded though, I was much more calm than the first time. I knew I had what mattered most.

We joined the convoy of vehicles crawling down the hill on McCullough. My horse stomped his disapproval all the way down the hill. At one point he stuck his head out the back of the trailer and seemed to see the fire. He pulled his head back in and was much quieter after that. We pulled into the Kelowna Riding Club to find bedded stalls with name tags waiting. I was relieved to see other horses being unloaded, he wouldn't be alone. We went to register at the evacuation centre and luckily got a room that allowed pets. It was after 1 a.m. before we got to bed, cat yowling in the crate, dog quiet and big-eyed with fear.

The next day we tried to get a pass to rescue our sheep and take them back to Lumby. The roadblock was only metres from our property but they wouldn't let us through. Instead we parked just down the road and watched the flames from a back burn, leaping up and devouring trees right behind our farm. It was a surreal experience, we could see the fire dripping from the helicopter and the trees just exploding into flames.

That weekend I took a trip to Lumby to visit my friend and herd some sheep for a bit of a break. I left hubby at the farm as we had been issued a day pass. As I headed home, I called and learned he had been waiting at the roadblock, chatting with the police officer there, for three hours and I was still another hour away. I hoped the officer was not going to time my trip from Lumby!

In the morning we heard that the fire had made it into the canyon and nearly wiped out our neighbourhood. The flames had stopped short of coming up our side and the danger was nearly over.

Tuesday we were allowed back home for the day. The sheep were okay, what a relief! A neighbour who refused to leave had been checking on them and filling the water trough. Then word arrived that we could stay. We went and got my horse, who was thrilled to see his home again.

For weeks after the end of the alerts, I felt lost, wondering what was wrong with me, why I couldn't just pick up and carry on. Months later, I still feel that icy grip when I see an emergency vehicle heading up my road. I think for me the most terrible experience of this whole fire was that somebody had the power to stop me from entering my own property. I was a prisoner on the wrong side, I wanted in. I have a new appreciation for the freedom we take for granted and a new fear of that freedom being taken away.

Chapter Ten
Human Nature
at its Best

"It was then that we heard a knock on our door. There was Pastor Mark Burch of Willow Park Church, saying that he had been able to line up some homes of his parishioners on the west side and he was checking with people in our condo to see if they wanted to leave for the night and feel more at ease."

JIM BAERG

"But as a phoenix arises out of its ashes, so did the life and vitality of the people. The valour of the fire crews, the compassion of local citizens, calls from faraway friends all told us we have much to be thankful for."

MARY B. JENKINS

KELOWNA FIRE CHIEF GERRY ZIMMERMANN'S STORY AS TOLD TO AND WRITTEN BY GLENNA TURNBULL

I guess at the beginning, we didn't really believe it would ever come here. It was so far away. We knew it was serious, but we thought it would be stopped before it reached the city. We found out that wasn't the way it was going to be.

When the lightning struck Saturday, a couple of trucks were sent in from Kamloops to help bolster what we had. We didn't really go looking for outside help until Wednesday when it began to look like it was going to get us. I'd flown over the fire on Tuesday afternoon, and it looked like it was heading towards Naramata and that they'd need the help, but that night, the winds changed and by Wednesday morning, guys were actually fighting it on Lakeshore Road. We had patrols out Tuesday night to watch, as flying embers can go quite a ways. Thank God we did because Wednesday was when we began to fight it full on.

On the Friday night when we were losing the homes, we had seven task forces (groups of five to ten trucks per force) out there when it blew up on us. We tried to get our people out to re-group at Barnaby Road but could only get four of the seven task forces out. One was stuck on Lakeshore and we had two others in the Kettle Valley area with their accesses cut off. In Kettle Valley, they'd been putting out spot fires when this big black cloud of smoke enveloped them without even knowing what had happened. One guy told me that as fast as they could run down the hill, that's how quick it was coming down at them. There were guys actually laying under the trucks throwing up. That passed, then it sounded like jet engines coming at them and the winds were coming so strong and the flames so high, they were looking at a three to four hundred foot high wall of fire. They had no where to go, their exit routes were cut off. Miraculously, nobody died. We only lost four homes in Kettle Valley. If those guys weren't in there we probably would have lost the whole subdivision.

It was a scary time. I thought we'd lost it all when they were cut off and couldn't get out. I dropped my head on the table thinking, "I've got dead guys up there, we've lost a good part of the city," it was the most helpless feeling I've ever had in my life that we couldn't reach in and pull them out. The only saving grace is that we had such good leadership up there, we had such good guys that if there was a way to get those guys out, they would and they did.

In the meantime, the commander we had on the hill phoned me to say we'd better start lining up bulldozers. This is when I learned what it was like to make hard decisions. If we couldn't hold Barnaby, this was going to come into the city and we'd have to start pushing houses down. That's the kind of decision that would take months and months to make under normal circumstances but we had to make that decision in a matter of minutes. So we started plotting on maps, figuring out where we'd have to do it and lining up the equipment.

While that was in process, we had that one hour period where we thought all was lost, then, miraculously, the rain came. It just dropped! You talk to different people and they say the firestorm causes its own weather. Others say it was just coincidence that it just happened. Then you figure, there were a lot of people out there praying. Was it divine intervention? I tend to think it was, but everybody makes up their own mind.

We all learned how to trust people. One of the neatest things was that no one questioned anything. The decision to bulldoze a path or put men in a situation was never second guessed, there was such a closeness of people working together, I'd never seen that before.

Probably one of the toughest things we had to do was telling people they'd lost their homes. We made a conscious decision right at the beginning to do two things: one, to take the media in as a full partner so the whole community would know what was going on; and two, that if somebody lost their home, we were going to let them know as soon as possible.

There was no text book to go to and find out how to handle this. We decided I would deliver the message, that it was my job to do, and that the church would be a good place to do it. The first houses were lost Thursday night and by Friday morning at 6 a.m., we had people out there already mapping out which had been burned and by 1 p.m., had the whole neighbourhood assembled in the Trinity Baptist church. We decided Pastor Tim Schroeder would say a few words, then I'd explain what had happened the night before, then read out the numbers of the homes by street.

One man got up and said, "I was watching from a distance. We were gone and your people stayed in there longer than I would have and it was my house. We hold no malice to you people, you did the best you could." Then they gave us a standing ovation. I still tear up when I think about it, just the way he did that, it set the tone for us for the whole thing. We didn't realize that morning that it was going to happen again that night.

The first night we'd lost 15 and saved 18, so we were able to deliver the news quickly, but the next night, when we lost 223, from several different subdivisions where a thousand homes or more could have been gone, it was different. I couldn't send my people up to catalogue it, so we had to get city planners, engineers out and they had to do up maps of what was standing and what was not. Sunday noon, we must have had 2,000 people in the church. We tried to sit them in neighbourhoods so neighbours could console neighbours.

Again, Tim started it by saying a few words. When I walked in wearing my red coveralls, it was a standing ovation. Knowing I had to tell these people whether their houses were standing or not, I got three standing ovations in about a three minute talk, telling them what we'd done, how we'd done it and

178

that we'd tried our best. It was the most unreal experience you could ever have. There was absolutely no anger towards us, it was the other way around.

We had about 65 different departments that came in to help us from across B.C. and even a couple from Alberta. They would all rotate crews – usually a crew of four or five – and they'd change every three or four days, so we had hundreds and hundreds and hundreds of people we worked with. Our management system was second to none. We had guys out there at staging that would set up which trucks went where. Everyone would be briefed and given a medical before they went out and again when they came in. If their blood pressure was up too high, we'd have to pull them off. We had psychologists here, too. A lot of guys felt bad after they came back and had lost all the houses, they felt responsible. We had to keep telling them, it's not what we lost, it's what we saved.

I stayed at the Fire Hall for six days straight during the worst part of it. There was maybe a total of ten to twelve hours of sleep that whole time. There was just so much adrenaline flowing that I didn't seem to get tired. Even when I did go lay down for a couple of hours, I'd just toss and toss. But when it was over and I did get out of here, I was tired for a month. It's funny what your body can do.

We held a press conference every morning to update the community. Every day they'd ask, is there anything you need? I had asked for support and suddenly, there were thousands of signs put up everywhere. We were getting palette loads of food and everything you could think of, we were inundated with stuff and lacked nothing. Sunday, we'd been through Hell and back for three days, and at the morning press conference, one of the other reporters asked, "Is there anything else you need?" I said, kind of off the cuff, "Well, I don't know about anyone else, but I could sure use a cold beer." I left the press conference and walked from there over to the Fire Hall, then someone came to get me, saying "hey, you've got to see this, there's a couple of kids outside." They came in, the cutest little kids, and they had this wagon with cookies, chips, a bouquet of flowers and a tub filled with ice and beer. I still have that tub. When I think about it, it still chokes me up. Little kids would come in bringing pictures and cookies they made me. I never got to see them all, but I did get to see a lot of them.

This one night, CTV was doing their news and this little girl with Down's Syndrome was out there with her mother and sister, and this special cookie they'd made just for me. I got right down beside her, we were completely surrounded by policemen, firemen, ambulance people and volunteers, and she gave me this cookie and I said, "Could I have a hug, I could really use a hug." Well, she gave me the biggest hug and kiss and everybody just broke down. The thing that got me was, here were all these people, doing what they could to help, and here she was doing what she could. It was so neat to have everyone pulling together for one common good.

A Lesson in Empathy
by Tracy Gray

Watching disasters and wars on TV and hearing about family member losses, although having feelings of empathy, is not the same as being through something similar. I realized that even with all of life's ups and downs, challenges and joys, my life had generally been smooth. August 22, 2003 and the weeks following have changed my life forever. I now know what "being in shock" feels like.

We left our house shortly before the evacuation order was given in our area in the Mission. We could see the flames approaching down the hillside and became fearful when the wind picked up, turning heavy smoke our way and blocking the flames from sight. The sound of helicopters circling and sirens was non-stop and we knew that was not a good sign. There were burnt pieces of bark the size of plates and full pinecones falling from the sky. Our four year old said, "Mommy, it's hard to breathe."

As we were preparing to leave, I kept thinking, "What can I not replace?" Pictures, a few important papers, our son's crafts he'd made since he was born and years of work saved on my computer's hard drive became important while everything else seemed irrelevant (well, there were those few bottles of older non-replaceable BC wines that made it in the van...). Our van was surprisingly not packed full.

We left our second vehicle so we could all be together. My husband put it into perspective as we were driving away by saying, "Everything important we need is here," and we both knew he was talking about the three of us. We saw neighbours packing up their vehicles and as we drove away, we noticed every vehicle was full of people and belongings. What amazed us was that we did not see any panicking. There were no vehicles speeding or road rage, there was only a calm exodus.

As we watched the fires burn from my in-laws, on Dilworth Mountain through the next few days, it was surreal. There were several of us welcomed into their home. Everyone helped each other in what way they could. We were all very gentle emotionally with each other as each was going through something different. Even with so many people sharing a bathroom, it was very amicable. Almost the whole houseful went to the Parkinson Rec Centre to volunteer. It was as if since there was so little control in what was happening, this was a way of doing something about it. We found it difficult to tear ourselves away from the TV or radio as things were changing so quickly we did not want to miss anything. For days it felt as if my whole body was numb and I was moving in slow motion. I was not alone.

I had just opened a new store exactly one month earlier and with little sleep, was working Saturday August 23. My business partner and some of our staff who were not supposed to be working that day came in to see if they could help and made sure we were all okay. It was really appreciated and made us all closer. All that day and for many days following, there were people trickling in, telling their own evacuation stories and also looking very numb.

There are parts of this experience that will stay with us. My son frequently says, out of the blue, that he is afraid of fire and thinks clouds are really smoke from another fire coming towards us. The sound of a helicopter triggers visions of smoke and flames that will probably stay with me a very long time. We were lucky. The whole experience was humbling. I realize what true empathy is.

Brianna's Hero
by Walter Dennison

There he stood atop a house roof, determinedly resolute, a saviour and hero in the eyes and heart of 11-year-old Brianna Neu. He and his firefighting comrades had saved Brianna's home while his own lay in ashes, devoured by the Okanagan Mountain Park Fire.

On that fateful night of August 22 on Curlew Drive in Kelowna, John Kelly fought unflinchingly during every second of duty, his mind devoid of his family's own loss because his entire being was focused solely on saving the homes of others.

"Everything seemed to be exploding as we ran down Curlew. We were in a dilemma – what do we do first, given everything was going at once. Flames were shooting out of every window and doorway."

In the end, though, John says proudly, "Our crew saved at least 10 homes for every one lost."

So, naturally, the 40-year-old firefighter's heart melted when Brianna presented him with her crayon drawing and poetic letter of gratitude. In his 21 years of service – nine as a volunteer and 12 on the force, no moment had so overwhelmingly touched John as when Brianna hugged him and handed over her creation. Brianna and John's daughter Meghan are best friends and classmates at Anne McClymont Elementary, and surely for as long as he's alive, John will joyfully flash back to that scene in the doorway of his parents' home, where his family had temporarily taken refuge. Eyes glistening, he smiled at Brianna's coloured images of a red heart and green hose, and large pink capitalized letters.

To: Mr. John Kelly, aka: my hero.
Dear Mr. Kelly,
When thunder & lightning struck in my neighourhood,
The fire was coming and on my roof you stood.
The fire was scary, and it came so fast,
the flames blew right past.
You must have been sad cause your house was gone,
but still, you saved my house and then moved on.
Because you and your partners lent a hand,
16 houses on my street still stand,
but if you hadn't been there,
there would be zero.

thank you, John Kelly, you are my Hero! (and also the other firefighters)
Yours truly,
Brianna Neu

John, his wife Gayle, and their children Jarred, Meghan, and Rachel, had been camping in Idaho since August 17. Over the next five days, John's ear was pressed to his cell phone several times daily, keeping posted of the situation both by his parents and comrades. Meanwhile, John's father, Mike, had transferred family photo albums and other treasured memorabilia packed by Gayle for safekeeping into his own home.

On August 22, four hours after deciding to return to Kelowna, the Kellys were motoring on the U.S. side of the border approaching Grand Forks, B.C., when John's cell phone rang. Comrade Scott Payer's voice was urgent: "When are you getting back?! Where are you?! Better get here fast!" John was told, tragically, of evacuations and evacuation alerts and how 15 homes on Rimrock and Timberline roads had been destroyed the night before when the raging beast leapt a 50-metre fireguard.

Three hours of speeding had the Kellys at Invermere Road, where John left the family and trailer at his parents' home, drove to the staging area, grabbed his gear and jumped aboard an engine headed for Curlew Drive. After two and a half hours of battling the flames, Lieutenant Al Chatham took John aside and gently broke the news, "Sorry, your house is gone." Quit fighting? Kelly sucked it up, appreciatively rejecting his comrades' concerns and continued fighting fiercely for another hour and a half. At 10 p.m., John took a short break and walked the few blocks to the remains of his home.

At 441 Trumpeter Road, John stood transfixed in shock. Reddish-glowing embers were all that whispered of a home levelled to its foundation. He thought: "What now? How do I tell Gayle and the kids?" Six houses up Trumpeter, comrade Rob Buchanan was also glaring at the shell of his home. Nine of the road's 16 homes were rubble.

Swallowing his sorrow, John questioned a firefighter hosing down hotspots. "There was nothing we could do, John, and you know we would have done everything to save your place."

Then, standing in his scorched yard, John braced himself while dialling Gayle on his cell phone. Sobbing, Gayle signed off bravely, "Take care, don't get hurt."

For the next four and a half hours, Brianna's hero battled on along Curlew until 3 a.m. Merely two hours later, the weary Kellys were at Parkinson Recreation Centre registering their loss.

Today, a gleaming new vision is forming over the ashes of the Kellys' tragedy – a splendid, new two-storey, stucco home designed to John's specifications. Move-in date is scheduled for mid-July.

Against the firestorm's larger outcome, John gratefully dismisses his own loss: "This ordeal has made us stronger. It has made us realize what's important in life. Material possessions can be replaced. Just think, nobody was killed! If we had lost anyone it would have been horrendous. Thank God we didn't."

THE SUMMER OF SMOKE
BY KEN THOMPSON

This summer was terribly different
the heat baked with not a respite
the lakes and rivers were the lowest in years
with no cooling weather in sight

Then the forests, some dryer than tinder
like a ticking bomb did explode
some from the lightning of nature
and some from a butt by the road

Now we cannot sing enough praises
of our fire crews on the front line
for it's there on the ground and up in the air
they're there for your good and for mine

It's dirty and dangerous hot slugging work
fatigue and heroics are part of each day
and along with the homes and the things that were lost
two aircraft went down that's the price that some pay

So these are the times we step up to the plate
and we do what we can to help out
providing a meal or a place to bed down
because that's what compassion's about

It's in times of disaster that bring us together
society's borders are crossed
businessman, tradesman, housewife or student
all give without counting the cost

And no matter how brave new beginnings,
they are very tough times and no joke
and none of us here will ever forget
the summer of trauma, heartbreak and smoke

Human Nature at its Best
by Pat Larson

Like most people in Kelowna, August 22 is a day we will never forget.

The day the fire started, my husband Earl and I had helped my sister Lorna and her husband Bruce pack up photo albums, etc., as they were on evacuation alert. Then on Aug. 18 they were evacuated from their cherished log home on Timberline. On the night of Aug. 21, the Okanagan Mountain Park Fire claimed 15 houses on Timberline, Rimrock, and Lakeshore Roads. The next day, Aug. 22, the residents of that area were asked to come to a meeting with city personnel and fire officials to learn if their homes had been among those lost. I attended that meeting with Lorna and Bruce, and sat with them while they learned the news they had been fearing.

I was so impressed with the people from that neighbourhood. Without exception, those who learned their homes were saved, while obviously relieved, were supportive of their neighbours who had lost homes and had the sensitivity to realize that some among them were devastated and in shock. At the same time, those who had lost their homes were genuinely happy for those who had not. I thought I had seen the best of human nature, but there was more to come.

My sister came back to our house with me. Her husband and mine arrived home from work and we sat together trying to digest the news their home was gone. We made plans to start a list of items to pack up in case my husband and I had to evacuate, because the fire was visible from our home in Black Mountain by that time. We had barely begun when the police were driving up and down our road on the loudspeaker, telling us that we had to leave immediately. I looked in disbelief as my sister and her husband calmly began packing up our photo albums, etc. I said "you don't want to be doing this now", and Lorna said "it's over for us now, so we're helping you." Bruce joked, saying, "we're experienced now." Now THAT is the best of human nature.

Roadblock Relief and the Okanagan Sun
By Mary Margaret Amodeo

I volunteered to work at the roadblock on Hwy. 33 in the Joe Rich area. After being on the barricade for almost three hours turning people away, a vehicle approached us around 11 p.m. By this time we were tired, thirsty and hungry. To our great surprise, the passenger window rolled down and a great plate of homemade goodies was thrust out the window along with the wonderful words, "if you want a coffee or need a bathroom, we live just down the road."

The goodies were well received and we passed the "extras" onto the next barricade minders. In that time of turmoil, some lovely family took the time to bake and then deliver plates of goodies to the volunteers on Hwy. 33. Heartwarming, tummy filling and very much appreciated.

My husband and I were the equipment managers for the Okanagan Sun football team. During the fire, their home field, the Apple Bowl, became Camp Kelowna for the armed forces. We were asked if we could get some footballs for the guys to throw around in their 'off time' from firefighting and the Sun was happy to accommodate them. The forces accommodated the Sun by allowing us entry to use our clubhouse and practice area.

One evening while on the practice field, trucks loaded with firefighters returning to camp rumbled into the parking lot. As they drove by the Sun team, they all started hooting and hollering and giving the players the thumbs up. It likely should have been the other way around.

During the course of our combined existence, we got to know some of the soldiers better. They watched our home games when they could and cheered the Sun players. They left notes on our whiteboard and even helped fold our game laundry when they had time off. We invited the soldiers into our clubhouse to watch TV and relax a bit when off duty.

It was a great companionship that grew until the army left town and Camp Kelowna was gone. The Camp Kelowna sign is in the Sun weight room, a reminder of the summer when football players and firefighters shared the Apple Bowl playing field.

Leo Gebert of St. Hubertus Estate Winery's Story

As told to and written by Pamela Irving

The RCMP came and we were told to leave. It was the night of the firestorm that we lost everything – our house, our winery, were all burnt to the ground. It was very hard on the kids and Barbara, my wife. Our vineyard backs right onto Okanagan Mountain, so we could see the flames at the back of our vineyard and feel the heat. Most of the vines had smoke and fire damage; we lost our entire crop.

We stayed at friends in Vernon and in a motel for awhile and are renting a place while our house is rebuilt. While we were away, we expected the chickens would have been burnt alive, but when we got back, they were fine, walking around, pecking at the ground. The army had been feeding them. Barbara and a neighbour boy rescued some gold fish from where the pond was – they were swimming around in a little bit of mud. The animals seem to have been the strongest in surviving the fires.

Luckily, my mother was here from Switzerland at the time. I think hearing about it from far away would have been hard on her. You could get information about the fires around the world. In Italy, friends told us that they had heard on the news that all of Kelowna had been burnt to the ground. They were very worried!

The effects of the fires, losing all of our family furniture, memories and things that had been passed down through generations, were hard – hardest on Barbara.

We are rebuilding our winery and home but I think it will take at least a couple of years before everything seems normal again. The community and firefighters have been amazing. We have had t-shirts and posters made with a photo of the fire taken from the entrance of the winery with the caption "You think you're having a bad day?" It makes people laugh, but also think. We also launched two wines in honour of the firefighters. Proceeds from these items will go to the fire fund for people in greater need than us. It is our way of giving back.

My Hero
by Julie Belgrove

The lightning struck the mountain the night of August 15 and as we sat upon the hills of Ellison, we watched the flames growing at such a rapid pace our hearts were struck with fear.

My husband Darrell is a volunteer firefighter for the Ellison Community. He is also an Airport Operations Specialist, (firefighter/maintenance) for the Kelowna International Airport. He was on holiday from the airport the week the fire swept across the southern hillside. Instead of taking a vacation, Darrell chose to stay put as he remained focused and alert of the growing fire.

Darrell received his call to help at 6 a.m. Friday, August 22. I chose to evacuate our children to the coast. Our middle son, Bennett, was suffering headaches and I, being a little on the claustrophobic side, was craving some ocean air. We were on the road by 4:00 p.m. and by the time we reached Coquitlam, the calls had already reached my in-laws that our neighbourhood had been evacuated. Through numerous calls and the support of our neighbours and friends, a few valuables and our remaining pets were rescued to loving homes. I had packed one bag of important papers and photos, the dog and the children. Everything else was just stuff.

We heard from Darrell, calling from a cell at the fire line at 10:30 p.m. that evening. He told me not to come home. He slept at the fire hall and was on duty again by 6 a.m. the next morning. Friday he was stationed in the Belcarra neighbourhood when the fire swept through the ravine and up the embankment toward the homes. The force of the wind from the fire blew the water back at them as they fought to keep the fire from reaching the homes. They worked feverishly in their wet gear, truly not concerned with their own safety. Saturday they were stationed in Crawford. Time stood still as I waited by the phone that day. Finally, at 12:30 a.m. Sunday morning, the call came in and once again he was safe. I returned home without the children that morning. We felt blessed to have two hours together before Darrell had to leave for the fire hall. In his hoarse voice, he updated me on his experience, explaining how at one point, they had no where to go, adding, "but if we had left, we would have lost some homes, so we waited it out until the fire passed by us."

Our holidays were spent in a very memorable way this year. I know in my heart there was nowhere else my husband would rather have been. His heart is that of a true hero. Not because he fights fires – that is just his job – but because he is brave and has a desire to save. Those are the qualities of a true fireman! I find myself still in tears telling our story. I am so proud of my husband, my fireman, my hero.

The Illusion of Control
by Lt. Howard Hisdal

First the police car turned on its siren and lights to get our attention, then: "You are under an evacuation order! Get out now!" The police cruiser moved on. It was Friday, 22 August 2003, the night of Kelowna's great firestorm.

Since Wednesday, I had been the Rear Party Officer for the British Columbia Dragoons (BCD), the local militia regiment in the Okanagan. My unit had sent soldiers to the Barriere-McClure fire the previous week and had just been given the mission of providing the headquarters for Task Force 2 (BCD). This task force was formed to fight the new menace of the Okanagan Mountain Park Fire. Our armoury in Kelowna was the site of the headquarters of the 500-man force and the Apple Bowl was the barracks for the one regular force and three militia companies of firefighters.

My wife and I live on nine-and-a-half acres of land on the Belgo Bench just across Mission Creek from Gallagher's Canyon golf course. One arm of the forest comes to within one hundred metres of us. We had an excellent view of the fire from its start on Saturday, 16 August. On the Friday of the firestorm I was working in the orderly room in Kelowna. My duty as Rear Party Officer was to keep track of the British Columbia Dragoons and to assemble more groups of soldiers for reinforcements. I was answering the telephone, receiving emails and checking the printer and fax machine for orders, delivering messages to the commanders, all the while listening to the local radio station and looking out the window from time to time into the grey shroud of smoke. We had lost fifteen homes that Thursday night and the Kelowna fire was now the top priority for the country. I listened with growing concern as the fire jumped one defensive line after another. Around four in the afternoon an evacuation alert was issued that included my home. I went to see my Commanding Officer, Lieutenant Colonel Denis Cyr, who was the commander of Task Force 2. He told me to go home and look after my family.

My wife had given birth to our daughter, Anna, only four weeks before and was recovering from surgery. We also had my wife's 87 year-old grandfather living with us. The smoke was clearing, a bad sign because it meant the winds had picked up. We could see the point of the fire less than ten kilometres away. The flames were way over the height of the burning Ponderosa pines. It was a class-six firestorm and it was headed our way.

I got everyone to pack a suitcase of clothes. We still did not really believe that we would be evacuated. I decided not to attempt to move furniture. We took some sentimental things. One thing was a piece of art made by my wife's mother who had died slowly of cancer some ten years ago. My wife pointed out the inscription on the back, "For my future grandchild." We had thought we could not have children and in the fourteenth year of our marriage had had our first child. Reading the words brought tears to my eyes. I hugged my wife. Out our picture window I could see police cars working their way through the orchard roads of East Kelowna below us.

When our turn came to evacuate, night had fallen and the flames resembled the gates of hell. There were people parked along the road above our vineyard looking at the fire. That irritated me immensely. Finally we were ready to go. My wife and child were in the lead in the car, then me in the truck with our two dogs, and then grandpa in his camper van. When we got to Springfield Road there was a long column of refugees. Then an amazing thing happened: traffic parted to let us through. It still brings tears to my eyes to think of it today.

We continued north to Winfield where a friend of ours gave us refuge. Her house was just out of sight of the flames. The next morning I went to the Parkinson Recreation Centre to register my family as evacuees. Then I drove on to the armoury to put in another day as the Rear Party Officer.

What I learned from the fire is that I can walk away from all that I own. It is people that matter, not things. I also see now how fragile humanity's place on this earth is. We think that because we can see something on television that we can control it. We do not have control; we have the illusion of control.

Unsung Heroes

by Tom Soames

I remember waiting for the call. Most of our heavy equipment had just finished up on the fire at Osoyoos. It was a matter of time to see how the fire progressed and if we could get the "big iron" in.

When the call came in, my first shift was to be through the night. I was supposed to meet my Cat at Gillard Main just above Kettle Valley Estates. A staging area had been set up there that, in later days, was evacuated and burned when the fire turned. When I arrived at staging, I found out my Cat had been dispatched earlier in the afternoon over Chute Lake Road to Naramata. Paradise Ranch was in need of more equipment as a section of the fire was moving in that direction. Back in the truck and down the highway was the only way there as the fire was now leaping in all directions, not making Chute Lake Road an option.

As I approached Summerland I could see the huge plumes of smoke across the lake. I was reminded that fires are a lot like bears: the only predictable thing about them is their unpredictability. Finally reaching Naramata's RCMP checkpoint and staging, I was sent to find my Cat at Paradise Ranch.

The pungent odours of wet and dry smoke were on the back of our throats and in our noses. Ashes in our eyes, soot everywhere, this is a pair of clothes that may never see the laundry machine again. The long and the short of it was, we defended at Paradise Ranch and the ranch was spared. Sometimes it goes your way and sometimes it doesn't. We didn't get noticed much because of all the activity on the Kelowna side. None of us are bothered by that, we just did what we usually do every summer when the fires come. They're usually miles up some logging road, so far from the smallest town that we're only seen as part of the statistics on the evening news. Heroes? Nah! Just regular guys.

After the fiery beast had been put to rest it became apparent that the devastation and scars did not apply just to the land, but also to the spirit of the people. It seemed sudden that I had switched from fighting this thing head on to now riding on its tail, hacking away at its remains. There I was, working in a symphony of excavators in Crawford Estates. One by one, the excavators would move from address to address: Westridge, Parkridge, Curlew, Okaview, Lakeshore, Timberline… the list went on, seemingly to never end. Scroungers sometimes preceding my arrival had already taken all the copper plumbing to sell at a scrap dealer: 40 cents a pound for burnt copper.

On my first day, I saw a woman standing in her living room staring out the window, hand over mouth. Her neighbourhood taken from her, I thought, her children's friends gone for a while. I think she was at that window all day. I met most of the owners of the homes I worked on. I had the privilege of working beside them, watching them sift through ashes as if sifting through their souls, a time of healing. In weakness and brokenness, without strength, they persevered. Not once did I hear a complaint, only comments of how fortunate they were.

Sometimes God tests us by fire. There was talk of rebuilding from those who lost their homes and from those who remained. But the people weren't talking about rebuilding structures, they were talking about rebuilding community. You could see it in their eyes and their spirit. Healing was in its infancy, but it would take longer than it took the fire to ravage them. Heroes? You bet!

GLOSSARY OF TERMS

ASH PIT: Powdery residue left behind when organic material is completely burned, such as a tree stump.

BIRD DOG: The term given to the command and control of aircraft. In the case of a fire, the bird dog aircraft co-ordinates the air part of the attack along with the firefighters on the ground. One of their roles is to determine the best routes in and out of the fire area and to recommend placement of fire retardant and water bucketing.

CANDLING: Candling occurs when the foliage of a tree or clump of trees ignites and flares up, usually from the bottom to the top.

CASTANET: A website in Kelowna that provided detailed updates and pictures on the OKM fire.

DUFF: The partly decayed organic matter on the forest floor.

EVACUATION ALERT: Residents are given either a written or verbal warning of potential evacuation. An evacuation alert can request that you be prepared to leave your home or place of business within minutes.

EVACUATION ORDER: Residents are instructed to leave their homes or places of business immediately. This is found in Section 115:1 of the Forest Act and Section 25 of the Fire Services Act. In Kelowna, many people were placed on "order" without being placed on "alert" due to the volatility and rapid spread of the fire.

FIRE STORM FRIDAY: August 22, 2003 was called Fire Storm Friday when winds of up to 90 km per hour moved the six day old OKM fire through the subdivisions of south and east Kelowna.

190

FIREGUARD: A barrier of cleared or ploughed land intended to check a forest or grass fire. Natural firebreaks include roads, ponds, cultivated fields, and rivers or streams.

FIRE LINE: A trail or trench dug down to mineral soil to control the fire.

HOTSPOTS: Large or small areas within the fire zone that need immediate attention either by air or from the ground.

MY HERO ROSE: The name of a rose bush that Byland's nursery in Kelowna sold to raise money for the BC Fire Relief Fund. A rose bush was given to each family that lost its home in the fire.

RANK SIX FIRE: A rank or category six fire is the most serious and violent category of fire activity. Its characteristics include crown fires, spot fires, fire balls and whirls.

SPOT FIRES: A fire started in advance of the main fire from embers or sparks propelled by the wind. Spot fires were noticed up to 2.5 kilometres ahead of the main OKM fire.

STAGING: Available personnel and equipment resources are held in reserve at a location away from the incident while waiting for their assignment.

STAND DOWN: A command for firefighters and army personnel to cease proceeding in the course of actions they were undertaking to wait for further instruction.

**All profit from *Touch the Flame* will be donated to
Camp Dunlop Restoration Fund, Canadian Red Cross Disaster Relief Fund
and Mennonite Disaster Service (Canadian Projects).**

Camp Dunlop Restoration Fund was set up in September of 2003 immediately following the Okanagan Mountain Park Fire. Located in the south Mission area of Kelowna, the camp's 30 acres of natural habitat were destroyed in the fire along with several camp buildings. Home to a number of Scouting and youth-centred programmes, the camp serves over 5,000 young people a year.

Canadian Red Cross is a volunteer based organization, serving Canadians since 1896 and focused on one goal – to improve the situation of the most vulnerable. In the summer of 2003 the Disaster Services program was activated to deal with fires in the Louis Creek, Cranbrook, and Kelowna service areas. Almost 900 Red Cross personnel provided food, clothing, shelter, and ongoing psychosocial support.

Mennonite Disaster Service is a faith-based agency that responds to disasters by providing volunteer labour for cleanup, repair, and reconstruction of homes. Following the firestorms of August 2003, over 300 M.D.S. volunteers responded to disaster survivors in Barriere, Louis Creek and Kelowna, cleaning up yards, repairing homes, building five new homes, replacing fencing, and supplying hay for some of the ranchers.